THE
MIGHTY
SEED

Book Two

Inspirational Poems

by

ESTHER SCHULTZ CONNOR

The Mighty Seed

Trilogy Christian Publishers
A Wholly Owned Subsidiary of Trinity Broadcasting Network
2442 Michelle Drive, Tustin, CA 92780

Trilogy Christian Publishing/TBN and colophon are trademarks of Trinity Broadcasting Network. For information about special discounts for bulk purchases, please contact Trilogy Christian Publishing.

Trilogy Disclaimer: The views and content expressed in this book are those of the author and may not necessarily reflect the views and doctrine of Trilogy Christian Publishing or the Trinity Broadcasting Network.

Manufactured in the United States of America

10 9 8 7 6 5 4 3 2 1
Library of Congress Cataloging-in-Publication Data is available.

ISBN: 978-1-63769-024-6
E-ISBN: 978-1-63769-025-3

Dedicated To

MY BELOVED SON AND DAUGHTER
Wayne H. Connor and the late Jade Darlene Connor

and

MY PARENTS
The late Reverend Clinton Darrell
and the late Olga Marion Gwendolyn Schultz

and

MY SISTERS
Eunice Schultz; Viola Facey; and Grace Schultz MD

and

MY BROTHERS
Michael Schultz Sr; Clifton Schultz; and the late Samuel Schultz

and

MY NIECES, NEPHEWS,
and all other family members and friends
who showed me their love and encouragement
in this wonderful venture of publishing
the second book of poems God inspired me to write
during the pandemic of 2020.

—Esther Schultz Connor

Preface

The year 2020 has been a unique one of many changes in everyone's life. The pandemic involved social distancing and no traveling. It was in the solitude and life changes that my love of God's Word and poetry blossomed into a "storm" of poetry writing. Inspiration flowed, and in a matter of three weeks, I had been inspired to write over seventy-five poems. The reaction of family and friends to these poems went from tears to excitement, to worship and amazement. The response was quite overwhelming, and I felt impressed to have them published to share with the world.

After the first published book of these poems, I continued to receive heavenly inspiration to keep writing. Topics range from words of encouragement, excitement, comfort, hope, peace, enrichment, and strength. This is the second book of inspirational poems written during the pandemic of 2020. I took the time needed to ask friends and family what issues or concerns they were dealing with, which inspired many of the poems written. My goal in life is to encourage and help others to live the abundant life Jesus Christ brings, to enjoy a greater intimacy and closer relationship with God, and to live a power-filled life.

Each reader is sure to find a variety of real-life poetry in *The Mighty Seed Book Two* to fit their desires and needs. These poems are just one of the ways God is using to touch the hearts of everyone reading them during these difficult and challenging times. It is God's will that we are drawn closer to Him. *So read, enjoy, and be blessed!*

—Esther Schultz Connor

Table of Contents

Esther Schultz Connor

A Class Act

You loved God unashamedly,
You did not turn away
From the training, you'd received
The foundation your parents laid.
Sin's many doubts and failures
Tried vainly without success
To turn you from the God you served
From childhood, without regrets.

You trusted God, held on
In sickness and in pain.
You loved and studied God's Word
Till from earth, you slipped away.
You left behind a witness
Of what it meant to be
Someone who trusted God
Loved Him unwaveringly.

You touched the hearts of people
You'd never seen before;
From the time you entered
To the time you left
All spoke highly of you and more
They know you loved God, your heavenly Father,
From your demeanor, in a critical stage
You crossed their paths, a class act
A witness of, to live is Christ, to die is gain.

Esther Schultz Connor

A Hope and a Future

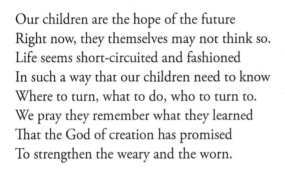

Our children are the hope of the future
Right now, they themselves may not think so.
Life seems short-circuited and fashioned
In such a way that our children need to know
Where to turn, what to do, who to turn to.
We pray they remember what they learned
That the God of creation has promised
To strengthen the weary and the worn.

Days of care, sorrow, and confusion,
Trouble and distress loom on every side.
Children do not know if they are coming or going;
They try to swim ashore, but it's against the tide.
Some search for an answer to questions
In some old pattern of use, previously laid.
It's a new day, time to reconsider their future
And to trust God for deliverance, and pray.

Let us remind our children, Jesus promised
That none would be plucked from God's hands.
These are the examples they should follow
To forgive, love, avoid the quicksand.
That would hold in its grip and sinking
If they refuse to believe and receive God's love.
The world may seem hopeless, to their thinking
The future's great; Jesus brought hope from above.

A Glorious Future

Time may be an enemy,
At times, it is a friend.
Sometimes it lags and languishes,
At times, hastening to end.
We yearn for the tomorrows
And speak of the might have been.
The God of creation is our everything;
On Him our lives depend.

We reach out and face the future
Mistakes we make along the way.
Thank God for His assurance,
He'll be with us every day.
It's a great mysterious universe
There's no beginning; there seems to be no end.
Skies withhold their glorious secrets
Our hearts hold eternity as a dear friend.

God keeps His secrets, for He knows
Our minds are too finite to understand
How God is Father, Son, and Spirit;
He has no beginning and no end.
He bids us come to Him as children,
Trusting what we cannot see.
By faith, we glimpse the future's mystery
Complete in Him we stand, believe.

Esther Schultz Connor

In the Holy Bible, it is written,
All who read will understand.
God prepared a kingdom for His beloved
The redeemed by grace, a holy band
Of believers, saints, their sins forgiven,
Adopted in Christ to a family divine.
We possess creation's promises:
One blood, one race, we inherit the land.

Till then, we face our future's destiny
Submit to life, the daily grind.
Within the hearts of God's own children,
A longing for deliverance lies
When time and death will be no more,
Only a glorious future in heaven as planned.
God's way is best; He holds our future
In His majestic, omnipotent hands.

A New Amazing Life

God, I'm coming home,
I'm so tired of the roaming
The distance from you only.
My heart yearns for your touch, Lord,
To see your face is my reward.
Just open the door and let me in,
I am tired of living with sin.
Can't wait for you to say,
"Come home, child, it's okay."

Father God, is that you I see
Running out to welcome me?
I don't deserve such love.
My squandered life, my innocence gone;
So many days of wandering alone.
I can hardly believe what I hear you say,
"Welcome, child, it's the dawn of a new day!
Once a Sinner, by grace, you're saved
To begin a new amazing life."

"You were never out of my sight, child;
I watched you day and night.
You know, I never slumber nor sleep;
Over you my watch I do keep.
I love you more than you know.
Can't wait to bring you home
Forever and eternity waits
You will rejoice as you enter heaven's gates
To begin a new amazing life."

Esther Schultz Connor

A New Life Will Receive

God my Heavenly Father,
My divine Daddy, you see,
So holy, kind and perfect
He wants the best for me.

When man free will was given
Satan tempted; our first parents sinned
By God's love, grace, and mercy,
Deliverance through Jesus Christ can be obtained.

Jesus my precious Savior, Deliverer
Gave His life on Calvary that day
His blood was shed, paid my sin debt;
He deserves all glory and praise.

Then the Holy Spirit descended
His power and presence from deep within;
Eternal life, victory, comfort was granted
To every believer who is set free from sin.

There is hope, joy, divine celebration,
There is a welcome for all who believe
And accept the free gift of salvation,
Righteousness and a new life will receive.

A Precious Reward

I give you thanks, Lord;
I give you praise.
I will worship you forever
Yes, all of my days.
Your honor and glory
Is my delight and joy.
My wonderful Savior,
Your love's a precious reward.

My beloved Savior and Lord,
It's you I adore.
No one can compare,
It's you that I live for.
You redeemed my life
Which Satan tried to destroy.
Your loving kindness, sacrifice
Brought tender mercies and more.

My tongue can't be silent,
You deserve all my praise
From now till forever
And all of my days
I'll worship your name.
My heart delights in you, Lord;
I'm so glad that you came
Your love's a precious reward.

Esther Schultz Connor

A Personal God

I may seem to be self-reliant, strong, and tough,
I take what life gives me; my God's love is enough.
His promises, His mighty power is perfect and true.
God stands near beside me in all I go through.

I may not cry, complain, or shed many tears.
My faith stands firm, for I know my God cares
The more hurt, pain, and sorrow that I feel
My God, He stands beside me; I want to do His will.

He is a personal God; on Him I depend;
His Words of promise prove He is my forever Friend.
God, my Heavenly Father, chose me for His own,
I bask in His love; He never leaves me alone.

He is the joy of my life, the dawn of each new day,
The sun, moon, and stars, a wondrous display
I face life with hope, faith, God's love, His presence
He is a personal God; He is forever my defense.

A Winner Here I Go

Here I go, don't you know?
My heart is fixed.
Satan, do not try your tricks!
Nothing that you deliver
Can ever compromise
This love I feel for Jesus
My everlasting prize.

Here I go, another day
The news may be just hearsay,
Trying to discourage me in some way.
I throw my head back high,
Look the devil in the eye:
Christ Jesus is my Savior;
His Words will last forever.
I trust Him fully, completely,
Don't need to ask Him why.

Here I go; my smile is wide,
Comes from deep down inside.
I'm walking through death's shadow grim,
I keep my eyes only fixed on Him
Who traveled this way a long time ago,
Faced Satan's tricks; in this world of woe,
Jesus knows the path I ought to take.
The way is narrow; make no mistake
Jesus loves me so much, this I know;
So here I go, a winner, here I go.

Esther Schultz Connor

A Wondrous Mystery

The heavens declare God's glory divine;
The firmament displays what we see.
We need heart, mind, and faith to believe
That God looked out on darkness and said, "light be!"
The miracle, the mystery of creation,
The universe God's power reveals:
One day His children, redeemed and knowing,
Will understand fully what they by faith now believe.

Our glorious, heavenly, majestic Father, God of all
Seen and unseen, God spoke and made
Us for His pleasure, beloved children to love and share;
We rejoice and celebrate just what He did
When minds are free, to will and do
Imaginations, dreams, pleasures fulfilled,
Such power unleashed, fully revealed
God knows, must be subject to His will.

Till then, we glimpse, long for a future unseen
A wondrous mystery God will fully reveal.
Love conquered children ruling the world,
Fully redeemed, contented, living in peace and joy,
Galaxies discovered; abilities now known,
Given free reign by God's Almighty hand.
Selfishness and sin can't enter, have no place
In the paradise of glory, now God's children understand.

Abound in Hope, Joy, and Peace

God will fill you with hope
When there seems to be no hope.
By the Holy Spirit's power
In the day or midnight hour;
Children of God abound in hope.

God will fill you with joy,
Joy that overflows with laughter.
Such joy by the Spirit's power
Every day and every hour;
Children of God abound in joy.

God will fill you with peace;
All this comes when you believe.
By God's power, you will receive
Such hope, such joy, such peace;
Children of God abound in peace.

Esther Schultz Connor

Accept God's Love

God's timing is perfect.
Have no fear,
Trust in His Word
He is always near.
Accept, believe His plans for you;
Jesus died and took your place,
Gave us the gift of mercy and grace,
Gave you the gift of righteousness too.

So, no shame, no fear,
Accept God's love.
It comes with messages from above;
Relax and lean on His mighty breast,
Join the joyous celebration with the rest.
The redeemed set free in Jesus name,
Once sinners, now forgiven;
Your life will never be the same.

This life is a preparation
For a glorious future divine.
Join the army of believers
In Jesus Christ, God calls mine.
The choice is yours to go to heaven one day;
Do not let Satan control your life, his way.
God sent you a big God hug today,
Accept His grace and mercy; you will be okay.
Let the Holy Spirit guide and lead your way.

Can you tell what will come tomorrow?
Or what the future holds for you and me?

Esther Schultz Connor

Will you lend or will you borrow?
Just believe and receive God's love; you will see
He wants the best for you; He loves you so!
Reach out and touch Him, then you will know
The joy, the delight only He can bring.
He is the ruler of everything
Accept God's wonderful love.

Answered Prayer

Answered prayer is like honey in my mouth,
Sweetness to my taste.
The tears I shed each night
They did not go to waste.
I called upon my God,
My Heavenly Father above;
He showered me with His presence,
His unconditional love.

So many times, my faith,
It wavered, at times, grew dim.
I prayed and called on God;
I related His promises to Him.
I quoted from the good book
Each verse I called my own.
My prayers rose like incense
To God's majestic throne.

The Holy Spirit deep within
My soul stirred hope so clear,
Reminding me each time
How precious I was, so dear.
The covenant signed in Jesus' blood
Was one no one could break.
God swore the truth, by Himself alone;
I am His child; He loves to answer my prayers.

As You Do
the Things You Do

You wake up very early
To face a brand-new day.
You smile and say, "Good morning!"
In your very own special way.
No one even imagines for a moment
How you tossed and turned in bed.
Visions, dreams, remembrances
Danced unhindered in your head.
Sprinkling seeds of distant memories,
Leaping barriers of stern control.
Sleep had relaxed your grip, your hold
Look closely; we may see into your soul.

Who has the time to listen, to learn,
How God helped you to make it through?
Many take for granted the strength you show
As you do the things you do.
God was there by your side,
Your protector and your guide
As you faced such hurts and pain.
Life knocked you down,
Your faith stood its ground,
Undefeated again and yet again.

You wonder if it's possible, how can you
Bypass that way, walking those miles?
There's nothing coming toward and against you
That you won't demolish, face with confidence, smiles;

Esther Schultz Connor

God did it once, two million, He'll do it again,
He's determined to see you through.
He's ever near; you have no fear
As you do the things you do.

Bless the LORD, O My Soul

PSALM 103

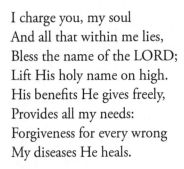

I charge you, my soul
And all that within me lies,
Bless the name of the LORD;
Lift His holy name on high.
His benefits He gives freely,
Provides all my needs:
Forgiveness for every wrong
My diseases He heals.

When my life like a flower
Flourishes like grass in a field
No one knows the day or the hour
God's mercy is all that I need.
Like a father, He shows
That if I listen to His Word,
His covenant He will keep;
O my soul, bless the LORD.

The angels excel in strength,
Listening to the voice of His Word,
Prepared His pleasure to do
His commandments to be observed.
God's mercy and grace, He pours out
On His children who fear
And remember His loving kindness,
Bless the LORD O, my soul, draw near.

Esther Schultz Connor

By God's Design

I am a sinner
Please help me, God;
I know you won't turn me away.
I am so far from perfect, Lord;
I went so far astray.
I want to come back home
To your loving arms today.
"Welcome home, my child,
Come on in, rest awhile,"
Are words I need to hear you say.

I am so tired of wandering,
Of feeling tired, being alone.
I need to see your smile, God,
As you tell me, "Welcome home."
I need to hear you say, God,
In your image divine, I am made.
Before my birth, you knew my worth;
By your design, God, my life You saved.

My heart is overwhelmed, God,
It yearns for your embrace.
The wanderlust has dried to dust,
I want to be home and safe.
This prodigal is home
Nevermore to roam.
I lay my head down to rest;
I feel so completely blessed.
God, your way is best.
I am loved, forgiven, by your design.

Catching the Air

I need to feel hopeful again.
I feel like I am catching the air.
The world seems to have turned upside down;
Nothing that happens seems fair.

My life was glistening with hope,
Then confusion walked in, wanting to stay.
How much longer must I wait for life changes?
Please hope, return home without further delay.

God really knows what I feel
As I deal with life's changes made.
I know, in the future, with God on my side,
I will be catching success, hope, and not the air.

Esther Schultz Connor

Children of Innocence

Children of innocence, sorrow, and pain,
Your eyes should be smiling,
Not filled with such shame.
You have no way to understand;
You are too young to know
Satan's the instigator
Demonic, destined for woe.

Pride-filled hearts need power;
Deprived, they settle for hate,
Cowardly seeking the weak
God's heartbeats, innocent prey.
Barbs of wickedness breeding self-doubt.
Confidence-deprived innocents, they say,
"Who can love me? What did I do wrong?
Why do I always feel this way?"

God, I know you see their sorrow.
God, I know you feel their pain.
God, I know the plans, your promise
To mend their broken hearts;
They're not to blame.

Father, soothe their wounded spirits,
Let them know they're not alone.
God of mercy, grace, and goodness
Where sin abounds, God protects His own.
God sees the tears, the fears, the footsteps,
Dread filling their hearts as raindrops fall;

Esther Schultz Connor

God dispatches unseen angels of hope,
Light beams of God's love, delivered to all.

Children of innocence, sorrow, and pain,
God sees, He hears, your whispers so clear;
God one day will wipe all your tears away,
The darkness will be over, no more tears.
No more tears, as you dance, celebrate;
No crying, no sorrow, in eternal day,
No night, no darkness, no footsteps of fear.
Children of innocence, dance around, celebrate!

Children of Tomorrow

Children of tomorrow,
Rise and raise your hands.
God calls you out for duty
You will inherit the land.
Carefree with laughter and friends
In the schoolyard, you once did play
It is time to face your calling
Hurry now; there is no time for delay.

Children of tomorrow,
We, your parents, stand with pride.
We worked hard to give you everything;
We will always be by your side.
There is one thing we must tell you,
So important for you to believe:
Take Jesus Christ as your Savior and Lord,
Let Him control your destiny.

We, your parents, suffered want;
Many days it shook our pride.
The lessons learned, as the years turned,
Was to have the Holy Spirit as our guide.
We believed the Bible as God's Holy Word,
We were not embarrassed to pray.
We put God first, come best or worst;
Children of tomorrow, the best is God's way.

Esther Schultz Connor

Chosen of God

A life full of such promise
With a welcome cry of "I'm here!"
I'm fashioned in God's image.
Look closely; His countenance appears
Unprepared for life's tears and sorrow,
Prepared for awesome pleasures, not pain,
Days of fun, happy feelings not borrowed,
Thank God for a family so dear!
They love me, I know
As days come and go,
Now prepared for today and tomorrow.

Some things are at best forgotten.
Undeserved, filled with sorrow and pain,
Life unloaded right upon my doorsteps;
I hope never to go there again.
Dancing in fields of remembrance,
Neatly archived, some stored with regret
For pain mixed with pleasure,
For tears filled with laughter;
Life's a mystery, just one chance we get.

Praise God for His Words of reassurance.
Nothing in this life can compare
With the glorious, delightful existence
He's prepared for all who believe to share.
He's provided a way of escaping
The doom selected by the sinner who waits.
Sweet surrender, relief, and rejoicing
For the chosen of God, His beloved saints.

Confident in Her Faith

What a wonderful blessing
There arrived on earth!
An Angel whose smile
Displayed her true beauty and worth,
Whose life was a treasure
To family and friends,
Who gave without measure
A love without end.

My mother was this woman,
Gentle and sweet,
Cared for her family;
Her love was such a treat.
Peerless in her generation,
As some may have heard,
Her epitaph, her victory,
She really loved the Lord.

She taught us from childhood
To read the Bible and pray,
To trust God for everything,
To thank Him and give praise,
To worship His name,
On Him totally depend,
To follow His leading,
Take Jesus as Savior and Friend.

What was her secret,
How on earth did she know

That to know God in His fullness
The Holy Spirit would show.
He would lead her and guide her
Every step of the way
All the way to heaven's portals
To live with Christ in eternal day.

Creation Groans

Creation groans in anguish,
Only wanting to be
The touch of love so tender,
Not the pain that we feel
For thorns and thistles
To caress, instead of giving pain,
To touch our skin gently
And bring sweet joy, not bitter tears.
Creation groans, awaiting, dreaming,
Wanting so much to share
A perfect world of wonder,
Peace and harmony everywhere.

The roses' sweet smell,
The lasting perfume,
The fireflies light,
Compete with the moon.
Darkness flees and hides,
Shadows will have no place,
The light of God's presence
Means eternal day.
The honeybees will offer
Their nectar so sweet;
Boys will walk on fences,
No harm to their feet.

The treetops soft cushion
Will bow down to greet you and me.
The lily pads offer
Padded seats as we kneel.

Esther Schultz Connor

We see mountains of splendor,
Peaks gleaming so bright
In the distance, the ocean's waves
Kiss the frames of soft sand
All around us, we see vistas
Of colors supreme;
The sweet smell of heaven
No longer a mystery.

Creation thunders,
Lightning flashes appeal,
The forces deep wonder
When will God's children be revealed.
Those former days of peace and joy
Harmony flowing among and between.
Nature, animals, and mankind
Were perfect, until sin and evil were seen.
Jesus Christ came down from heaven;
Seems Creation knew the plan.
Jesus died, brought grace and mercy,
It is finished, the Savior redeemed Man.

God the Creator, Heavenly Father
Has set the final day and the time
To settle all things created.
Perfect union, sublime
Time and death will be no longer,
Satan's doom in hell, final screams.
Creation also set free from Satan's diabolic schemes
Set free from bondage and decay,
Reveling in the glorious liberty,
The freedom and deliverance
To God's children then revealed.
God's children, Christ's blood made perfect
Creation's reality, no longer a dream.

Death Is Destroyed

Our enemy and foe you are.
Your destruction complete awaits
As we enter heaven's gates.
Drop our load of earthen care
Lightly mobile on our feet,
Death has lost its victory.
We float, we fly, with God's power, we are safe
Visions of rapture, saved by grace.

All dominion death has lost
When Jesus died upon the cross.
Saints redeemed, we rejoice and sing
March triumphant with our King.
Jesus crowned the Lord of all;
Christ Jesus won our heaven's reward.
Death, you're conquered, we're set free
To live forever in victory.

Esther Schultz Connor

Divine Love

Your divine love is so amazing
And how You make me feel.
I am inspired, delighted
Your love is oh so real.

You take my heart in Your hands,
Guide me along the way.
I never could imagine
The way I feel today.

It's mysterious, it's wonderful,
The touch of Your divine love.
The only way to describe it
Is that it comes from heaven above.

When I feel that I am lonely
I hasten to Your side.
Your presence, it enfolds me
There in Your love, I abide.

I cannot understand it
The love You freely give.
Jesus came to earth from heaven;
In His love, I abide and live.

It's mysterious, it's wonderful,
The touch of His divine love.
The only way to describe it
Is that it comes from heaven above.

Do Something

My grandmother's words I still remember:
So intense, so poignant, so sweet.
I had passed by her bedside that morning;
She asked me what I was doing,
I told her, "Nothing, just nothing."
This is what she said
With her eyes fixed on me:

"Do something to help yourself
And to help others too.
There's no time for you to delay;
There is work for you to do.
The harvest is past; summer is ended
The laborers are few.
Do something, my child, do something,
God is counting on you."

Her words of "do something"
Are words I live by today.
Grandmother is now up in heaven;
The world's in confusion and pain
Reminds me of Sodom and Gomorrah
And of Lot, that old times saint;
His soul was vexed by the wicked.
Did he do something any day
To help himself and to help others?
Why were there not even ten people saved?

"Do something, my child, do something."
I wake up with those words on my mind.

Esther Schultz Connor

The enemy of our souls, he's busy working;
He knows he's running out of time.
For our lives' destruction, he has a goal;
He knows there's no time to delay.
The harvest he wants to reap is our souls.
Grandma and I say, "No way, devil, no way!"
My life's goal is to do something for myself and others.
As Grandma said, there's work for me to do;
I remember her piercing eyes fixed on me,
Saying, "Do something, God is counting on you."

Do Your Dance

Another path, another chance,
Another day, to do your dance.
Sing hallelujahs to lift your voice
To glorify God's name, to laugh, rejoice.

Sing God's praises, lift Him high,
Shout His name up to the sky.
You're not shortchanged; it is a fact:
Jesus Christ the Savior has your back.
Angel armies stand ready, all prepared
To protect your life from Satan's snares.

God knows your name; He does not change.
You can trust His Word; He never fails.
Even when nothing seems to work out as planned,
Put your faith and hope in Him, take your stand,
Let grace and mercy lead your dance.

God the Father really knows best:
Might be a trial or a test,
Look deep down inside yourself;
Just trust in Him, and leave the rest
Take the path as Jesus leads.
Another chance for you to succeed,
Another day to do your dance,
Let hope arise; it's not by chance.

God's intentions are for your good,
For you to live life as you should.
So, take the plunge, hold on tight

Esther Schultz Connor

To God's outstretched hands, with all your might.
For your life, He has a wonderful plan
Rejoice in Him, and do your dance.

Don't Wait, My Friend

Do not wait until
Your light goes dim
And time steals your life away.
The games people play
Cause you such dismay;
Your thoughts in disarray.

Make wise decisions
While you can.
Don't wait until the time
Your mind wanders; it's a sign
You need to act quickly
Before you are left behind.

The Bible tells us clearly,
Now is the accepted time.
The day of salvation is here,
Or final doom and despair,
It is the time to make a decision;
The day of reckoning has appeared.

Do not wait until later,
The future is now.
Make your exit gracefully
As you take a bow.
God offers peace and love
Forever with the heavenly family above.

Do not wait, my friend,
Open your heart's door wide,

Esther Schultz Connor

Accept Jesus Christ as your Savior,
Let Him in to abide.
Joy unspeakable awaits;
Perfect love, now do not delay.

Enjoy His Love

When feelings and thoughts
Flood your soul with unrest,
You've done what you wanted,
Trying hard to do your best.
Just believe and receive
All His precious promises.
You are His beloved children,
Rest, relax, enjoy His love.

God loves you so much,
Sent Jesus from above
To reclaim and redeem
All who are His very own
Plundered by the enemy,
The enemy of our souls.
Seems we were lost,
Forgotten and alone;

But piercing the darkness
Hope's light streams appear.
God the Father of all His children
Removes all doubt, fear, and despair.
The battle you are fighting
Has already been won;
You are His beloved children,
Rest, relax, enjoy His love.

Jesus left His home in glory
To show us His divine love.
A wonderful love story

Esther Schultz Connor

Birthed in God's heart above.
Sit down and enjoy His presence,
Be humble, accept His deliverance,
You are His beloved children,
Rest, relax, enjoy His love.

Joy unspeakable,
Glories unimaginable
Await those who believe and receive His love.
Reach out and claim it,
Shout aloud and enjoy it.
Streams of mercy tell the story,
Rivers of goodness, love, and glory
Poured out on His children;
You are His beloved children,
Rest, relax, enjoy His love.

Every Moment
of Every Day

Mighty monarch, majestic Lord,
You deserve all my praise.
Your throne, your glory,
Your grace, a tender, divine love story
Enthralls my heart, my mind, my being, I'll praise you
Every moment of every day.

You gave me life and peace,
You gave me the air I breathe,
Among a billion souls, you let me sit
In heavenly places on high.
I'll praise your name till the day I die
Every moment of every day.

Thank you, God, my heart rejoices
In your great eternal plan.
You fashioned me in Your own image.
You are my God, the great I am,
My life is yours, your will I obey, and I'll praise you
Every moment of every day.

Esther Schultz Connor

Everything to Me

Lord, you are my everything,
Lord, you are the song I sing.
I want to fill my mouth with praise
And glorify your holy name.

When I face sorrow and pain,
Lord, you show me all I gain.
I want my life to reflect your glory,
I want to shine and tell the story.

Lord, you are all that I need.
I rest in you, Lord; please lead,
Be my guide close by my side
Night and day, show me the way.

Lord, you are my strength and shield,
You are my joy, my will I yield.
You changed my life so completely,
Your love means everything to me.

Express Your Love to God

Thank God for each new day,
Let joyful praise arise at creation's majestic display
The trees with leaves of green,
The skies of azure blue,
Their horizons kiss the earth,
Saying, "Hello, how are you?"

The flowers so multi-hued,
The rainbow's blend when viewed
Remind us of God's artistic talent, so great,
Was freely shown to man
Since this world, heavens and universe began,
Enticing us to call boldly on His name.

Suppose all things were colored red
Or black or white, no blend.
God knows the sameness on display
Would stifle talent's delight,
Combining beauty's boundless might,
Restricting release of joy and praises to His name.

Creation is only a taste
Of things God has for those who wait,
Trusting fully that God our Father knows best
That His children's inner desire
Fueled, unlimited, inspired
Are a reflection and reminder, God holds the rest.

Esther Schultz Connor

Fat and Flourishing

PSALM 92:12-14

So many promises God gave us
We reach out and take for our own.
In the Word, it so clearly is written
For the upright, gladness and light are sown.

The righteous, God said, like the palm tree,
Shall display such spiritual growth
That in the golden years of old age
Fruit they will still be bringing forth.

Fat as the goose for Thanksgiving,
Flourishing as one thousand flowers in bloom,
They will prosper in love with no limits,
The light they possess banishes gloom.

The sweet fat and the flourishing join together
To celebrate and to show that the Lord
Is upright and completes what He promises
Like a rock, we can depend on His Word.

We have tasted of the good life in Jesus
In our youth, many battles we waged.
Sweeter still are the blessings God promises
For the righteous and upright in their old age.

Fear Is Destroyed

PSALM 4: 8

Fear is a monster,
A fiend that grows,
Bullies all in his path,
Like a sower, he sows.
Sprinkles hate, self-loathing,
Like the dew on the ground.
You tiptoe around gently,
Your footsteps make no sound.
In the still of the midnight
No sound could be heard.
Your screams fall on deaf ears,
For you have not uttered a word.

Your screams are internal,
Locked deep down inside.
Torment flows unhindered
A far-reaching tide
Of emotions and heartaches,
They are given no voice.
They learned to be silent,
To be still and not rejoice.
Keep walking and talking,
Fear's controlling design,
Determines to subdue slowly,
You heave a soft gentle whine.

When suddenly, was that the doorbell?
Hope's chimes ring loud and clear,

Esther Schultz Connor

Dispelling fear's stronghold,
Defeating doubt and despair.
The Herald of mercy
Of hope, peace, and love
Descends softly, gently,
God's messenger from above.
You belong to your Father,
He fashioned you like Him.
His voice was soft and gentle
Yet piercing within.

Doubt and failures in a moment
Fall swiftly with no sound.
The Creator had spoken,
Love beams circle around,
Enveloped by God's presence.
You stand straight and tall,
Your Words of victory
Demolish those walls
That held you as captive.
God allowed no defeat;
You are destined to win,
So, celebrate your victory!
Fear is destroyed.

Find My Way Home

I am wounded beyond recognition:
Why did God leave me here?
What good am I in this world?
I have nothing left to share;
I used to walk tall, unaided,
Took care of my needs alone.
Now here am I, a shell of who I was,
Trying to find my way home.

What gifts do I have to offer?
On whom can I lean and rely?
Who sees me as I used to be,
A strong person not afraid to try?
The way ahead is fraught with danger;
I will try to make it on my own.
Dear God, you left me here,
I need your help to find my way home.

My heart sings, I cannot be silent,
My hope lies in God's Holy Word.
He promised to strengthen the weary;
I fight on to gain love's reward.
I hear the Holy Spirit whisper,
"Have faith in God, trust Him alone."
God knows the path for me to take;
His love will guide my way home.

Esther Schultz Connor

Follow God's Plan

When early in the morning I arise
To face a new dawn, I pray,
"Lord, I come to you today
With a thankful heart, I give you praise,
With great gratitude, I must say
You've helped me along the way.
From before my life began
You chose me and had a plan.
You placed me in a family so dear,
My precious mother, her heart full of love and praise
Showed me, Jesus, to her it was so clear,
Success in life is to follow God's plan."

God's plan He revealed
John 3:16 is clear.
God loves the whole world, gave His Son;
Believe and receive
Life everlasting, draw near
For success in life, follow God's plan.

Many problems I had to face,
Struggles and trials that took place,
God helped me to run the race,
Forever I will give Him praise.
For before my life began
God chose me and had a plan,
I gave my life to Jesus at an early age;
Satan determined a war he must wage
To wrest my life and soul from God's hands.
Foolish, immortal, impossible task:

Esther Schultz Connor

My future is settled, God holds me fast;
I want success in life, so I'll follow God's plan.

God's plan He revealed
John 3:16 is clear:
God loves the whole world, gave His Son;
Believe and receive
Life everlasting, draw near
For success in life, follow God's plan.

Food for My Soul

I drink to quench my thirst,
I walk a dry, barren land.
The desert of decisions
Face me on every hand.

I eat the bread of sorrow,
At times I face pain and grief.
I lift my voice to God on high,
"Please send me some relief!"

"Drink, child, from the water of life,
You will never thirst again.
The bread that you eat meant Satan's defeat;
Jesus' broken body was part of My plan."

"My word, it feeds your soul
Like honey-sweet nectar to taste;
Jesus' blood makes you whole
Come buy without money, make haste,

"Accept the free gift of righteousness
For your sins, on the cross, Jesus died.
All my believing children are blessed
Because My Son, your Savior, was crucified."

I shout and dance, I praise
Almighty God, my Heavenly Father on high.
What love, what mercy, what grace!
I am blessed, redeemed, delivered, satisfied.

Esther Schultz Connor

God Is Great and Greatly to Be Praised

PSALM 96:4

GOD
God the Supreme Creator,
Our eternal, heavenly Father
IS
Is the great I AM,
The awesome gift-giver
GREAT
Great is His name;
Power and Majesty belong to Him
AND
And everything we need
He provides and more
GREATLY
Greatly magnificent
That's why our God we adore
TO BE
To be completely known is His promise,
We can trust His precious Word
PRAISED
Praised both now and forever,
Shout hallelujahs, He is LORD!

God is great and greatly,
So greatly to be praised;
His love is poured out freely,
All glory and honor to Him we raise.

Esther Schultz Connor

God our heavenly divine Father
Deserves our gratitude and praise.
God is great, oh so greatly,
So greatly to be praised.

Jesus Savior for our sins was crucified;
The grave and death could not hold Him.
The Holy Spirit's power was magnified,
As Jesus rose triumphant, giving us power over sin,
He rose, gave us His righteousness
It is freely given to all who believe.
No one is denied who accepts His lovingkindness;
Grace, mercy, and forgiveness they will receive.
Our God is great, and oh so greatly,
So greatly to be praised.

God Is Our
Refuge and Strength

PSALM 46

God is our refuge;
In His strength we trust.
When trouble comes our way,
His help delivers us.
His children need not fear,
Although earth and mountains shake,
And be carried into the sea
The troubled waters roar and rage.

The city of God, the holy place
Of the tabernacle of the Most High
God Himself stands in her midst
The river, streams are flowing by.
The Lord of hosts, Jacob's God,
Our refuge, in Him we trust.
He makes wars on earth to cease
Our God will surely help us.

God is our refuge,
He is our strength,
He asks us to be still,
To know that He is God, our defense;
Creation does His will.
He makes wars to cease
Upon the earth, we wish for peace.
God is our help, refuge, and strength;
His Word is true; in Him we believe.

Esther Schultz Connor

God Knows

No need to worry,
No need for anguish,
No need to hurry,
My fears, they vanish.
God has the answer
He will reveal,
God knows and sees,
His love is real.

God knows my heart's cry,
My deepest need;
God knows my sorrow,
My pain He feels.
His love surrounds me,
His joy He gives me.
By Him, I am set free,
By Him, I am redeemed.

Jesus Christ is the reason
For the joy I feel inside.
No matter what comes my way,
In His love I trust and abide.
Although the news we hear
Seem to offer little hope and peace,
God promises to deliver His children;
God knows His perfect ways we believe.

God knows the future;
For my life and yours, He has a goal.
Trust in His promises;

Esther Schultz Connor

Will calm a worried soul.
He knows what is best,
He still is in control.
Just breathe and enter His rest
So reassuring, God knows.

God Knows the Reason

Whose fault is it, mine or yours?
Did God the Father set this up,
Made me drink from this bitter cup,
Or is this some evil Satanic lure?

The reason may not be clear,
My destiny is secure.
God will work all these things out;
For my good I'm very sure.

The reason at times I cannot fathom,
How did I arrive here from there?
Thank God I know He will keep me
Even when these things appear.

The choices I make on occasion
Are not always the best, I agree.
Is it God putting me to the test?
Or some mysterious reason, unknown to me.

The reason may not always be clear,
My destiny is secure,
God will work all these things out;
For my good, I'm definitely sure.

In the book of life, God reveals
Those who trust in Him are sealed.
Does not matter, come what may,
God the Father has the final say.

Esther Schultz Connor

He'll reveal all things when He appears;
God knows the reason,
Then He'll make it absolutely clear.

God Promised Good

JEREMIAH 32:37-42

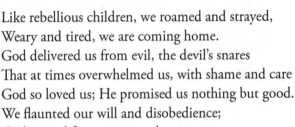

Like rebellious children, we roamed and strayed,
Weary and tired, we are coming home.
God delivered us from evil, the devil's snares
That at times overwhelmed us, with shame and care
God so loved us; He promised us nothing but good.
We flaunted our will and disobedience;
God waited for us to come home.
The welcome received, we did not deserve it,
God's goodness and mercy forever will flow.

God promised good,
We did not deserve it.
He welcomed us home
With such love and forgiveness.
The light in the window,
The hearth blazed a welcome;
God's promises are so good.

God said in His mercy we are His people;
God made a promise; He is our God
Of one heart, one way was chosen
To fear and to love God, as we should.
God promised us good and our children after
To do us good, and to never turn away.
Imagine God, with His whole heart and soul
With all power and majesty, angels under His control,
Rejoicing over us, assuring us, gave us His Word.
This life is a beginning, eternity our reward
He promised us nothing but good.

Esther Schultz Connor

God Rules Over All

JUDE VERSES 1-25

Your behavior matters to God,
Your own desires you must submit.
You must strive to do His will,
To honor Him and not resist
To remember the things you have learned
Of His faithfulness and truth.
Such works will reap a reward;
The fire will burn hay, stubble, and wood.

Present your body to be sanctified,
Build yourself up in your most holy faith,
Praying in the Holy Ghost as inspired,
Looking to Jesus, as for Him you wait.
Keep yourself in the love of God,
Have compassion on others with fear,
Pull them in haste out of the fire,
Faultless in God's presence, one day you will appear.

To all by God the Father sanctified,
You are preserved in Christ Jesus and called
Mercy, peace, and love to you are multiplied.
God the Father rules in wisdom over all.
He is able to keep you from falling
And present you before His glory with great joy
To God our Savior, who alone is wise,
Be now and ever majesty, dominion, and power.

God Says Come

Come those of us so wounded
By life's trials and its thorns.
God made the world most beautiful;
Man's choice entangled all.
So wounded hearts, you're welcome,
Lay your head in His mighty embrace,
Close your eyes, enjoy His presence,
Someday you will see Him face-to-face.

Come those of us with scarred hearts.
The enemy's defeated, Jesus reigns;
His majestic arms are open wide
For those who need a friend.
He sticks much closer than you dare hope,
He Is so real and knows your pain.
You are created in God's image,
Jesus the Savior took away your shame.

Come weary ones and broken,
Hearts aflame, though petrified.
Will the God of grace so holy,
Will He welcome or deny?
The Holy Bible tells us truly,
We are His children, to Him belong;
All who confessed believed in Jesus
The Holy Spirit in your heart places a song.

Come wounded, scarred, weary and broken,
Lean against His spear pierced side.
No matter what, when, where it happened,

You are welcome; Satan lied.
God will soothe and comfort prodigals,
Yearning for peace, He'll welcome them home.
The fatted calf will be the victim;
You're in God's family and never alone.

God's Beloved Lamb

1 CORINTHIANS 6:20

"I am not my own,"
I read in the Holy Word.
If not my own, then whose?
I belong to Jesus Christ the Lord;
He bought me with a price,
Shedding His precious blood,
He took my sins away,
And bought me back that day
My Redeemer, the beloved Lamb of God.

I live life by His grace;
His mercy overflows.
I run this daily race,
He leads me where I go.
He knows the path I take,
My life is in His hands.
His will is my command,
On His precious Word, I stand—
My Redeemer, God's beloved Lamb.

All glory, honor, and praise
To Jesus Christ my Savior, I raise.
He knew no sin; from heaven to earth He came.
The glory He had before
By the Angels, worshipped and adored,
The King of Kings, the Son of Man His name.
My life's now so special; my name is sealed
In the book of life, ready for reveal
By my Redeemer, God's beloved Lamb.

Esther Schultz Connor

God's Other Name
Is Not "By Chance"

So many miracles happen,
Things no one can even explain.
The unknown becomes the known
When fate and chance seem to become the same.

"How on earth could that happen?"
You question, doubt, try to explain.
Things could have worked out another way
When by chance, things lined up your way.

God's timing is impeccable;
He hears, sees, and knows it all.
The affairs of His children are before His eyes, on display
Not by chance, God will be coming soon to call.

You pray for an answer to a problem,
You need for it to happen today.
Your trust in God never wavers;
Others, by chance, is not your God's other name.

Watch God arise in His mighty splendor,
Angels hasten, His will to obey.
The time and tide that wait on no man.
Halt in midstream, by chance? No! it is what God says.

God's Wonderful Love

My life is like a movie,
Begun in black and white.
I exited that birth tunnel
To a wonderland so bright.
A sweet smiling face
So near for me to see,
Kisses and caresses,
Gentle warm hugs just for me.

I joined a family
To love and care for me.
They protected me, kept me safe;
I grew so rapidly.
I learned of God's wonderful love,
The love He had for a sinner like me.
He sent His Son Jesus to die for me
Because of His wonderful love for me.

The Bible tells this love story
How Jesus left His home in glory.
God, the Father's voice was loud,
It echoed through the clouds.
"This is Jesus, my beloved Son
In Him, I am well pleased."
From sin, Jesus set me free, to join a new family
Because of God's wonderful love for me.

Esther Schultz Connor

77

Good Times, Bad Times

Let us seek Him in the good times
As much as in the bad times.
He deserves more, much more than we give Him.
We get down on our knees,
We shed tears, and we plead
Pain and sorrow touch our souls deep within.

Why do we not show God
The love He deserves.
All the praises, all the worship
Just because He is Lord.
Daily offer our love to our Father above
Just because, just because He is Lord.

Let us seek Him in the good times,
Let us seek Him in the bad times,
Let us seek Him in sorrow and pain,
Just the same, even more,
In the sunshine or when it rains,
Just because, just because He is Lord.

God deserves all the love
That He gives freely from above.
Returned to Him, He deserves so much more!
Let us love Him in the good times,
Let us love Him in the bad times,
Just because, just because He is Lord.

Our loving Heavenly Father deserves more,
Much more than we offer to Him.

Esther Schultz Connor

Forgive us, Lord; we give our word
To faithfully adore you, just because
Our hearts overflow with love for you,
Not only because you do
All the wonderful things you do,
Just because, just because you are Lord.

Her Final Words

Tears filled my eyes;
It came as no surprise
Mom's health was fading fast.
How much longer would she last?
Her life had seen many years
Of laughter, joy, and tears.
Mom knew Jesus Christ as Lord and Savior;
She was ready to live with Him forever.

Her final words were a sweet benediction;
I knelt close to hear her sigh and whisper,
"God bless you, child, let God take control,
Control your life, control your plans,
This night and the rest of your life."

This dear saint summoned all her strength and might
To speak a final blessing,
Give me words of advice
That would make my way prosperous
And grant me good success in life.
With great determination, she managed
To speak her final words in life
And to say, "God make my child a light,
A mighty blessing in Jesus Christ."

The memory of those moments
Soothe my heart and soul today
To think of my sweet, precious Mother
And what she had to say.

Esther Schultz Connor

She lived a life of service,
Of hope, love, faith, and charity.
A woman of God, who lived by His Word
A true saint, life void of hypocrisy.

His Majesty King Jesus

Your presence is cerebral,
Your presence is heavenly,
It is honey to my soul,
It touches deep inside of me.

It encompasses my entire being;
Soul and spirit become one.
Human beings taste the majestic,
Divine adoration of God's own Son.

No desire on earth can compare
With God's awesome Majesty.
Humbly I fall and kneel in His presence,
The one who died to set me free.

My heart is ablaze; the mystery
Of God's amazing love for me.
I can do nothing to deserve it,
Love unconditional that set me free.

Nothing on earth can ever compare
With God's love for eternity.
I must forever dwell in His presence,
All glorious, King Jesus, His Majesty.

I have been given by God to Jesus;
Jesus wants me to be with Him
In heaven to see His majestic glory
That He had before the world's beginning.

Esther Schultz Connor

Home at Last

We fasted, and we prayed;
At God's feet, we laid.
The pain in our hearts,
The tears that did start;
We blinked, held them back,
Tried another tack;
Was there any other way?
All we could do was to continue to pray.

The daily updates were grim.
We could not lose him,
His health and his cure,
We placed in God's hands, so sure
From his sickbed, a miracle would rise
And our praise would reach the skies.

The stripes on your back, Lord,
Meant our brother's healing was assured.
How little did we know,
From the beginning, it was so
God's plans were different, so much better
Than the ones we had made.
In His hands, our dear brother, we laid.

I imagined my brother touring heaven at the start,
Of the sickness, as the health team did their part,
The glories and the wonders of the heavenlies,
Surpassing his imaginations, visions, and dreams.
God's beauty, the angels, the saints, he would behold,
He would be walking, rejoicing, on streets of pure gold,

Esther Schultz Connor

He would need no walker, wheelchair, help, nor cane,
His limbs would be strong; leaping, jumping, without any pain.

The pure river of water of life, streaming from the throne,
Multitudes of worshippers singing a new song;
Mom and Dad, family and friends would be there,
Surrounding him, joy unspeakable, no sorrow nor care.
He would see King Jesus, our Savior, Redeemer, glorified,
Majestic, triumphant, in shining splendor, magnified.

To a bed of sickness, broken body, weakness, and pain
He had no earthly wish to return there again.
"Heavenly Father," I imagine he asked, "please can I stay?
If I could only have things my way."
"I am finally home; I have run my race.
Perfection is mine, by God's wonderful grace."

"Yes," God would say, "you are welcome in.
By my Son Jesus Christ's sacrifice for sin,
Upon that cruel cross, Mercy and Truth have met;
Here is the robe of righteousness and crown of life you get.
Righteousness and Peace belong to you; they are gifts.
You will be staying here now; I have granted your wish."

My brother would be dancing around with joy,
Shouting hallelujahs and praises to the Lord.
"No pain, no sorrow, today or tomorrow,
According to God my Father's Holy Word.
Goodbye, my dear loved ones; I will see you soon.
I am free, I am in heaven, at last, I am finally home."

I imagined God's welcome to my brother, all this and more.
So, until we meet again on that heavenly shore,
Goodbye, my dear brother, reunited with our precious mother,
Kiss my daughter for me, say hello to Dad and our baby brothers,
Until the time when we shout, hallelujah, death is past
And we are finally together forever, home at last.

The Mighty Seed

How Long Must I Lean on Mommy?

How long must I lean on Mommy?
Are her reserves of strength so many?
Must she still hold my hand
As her wrinkles grow,
And her gait is slow;
When will I understand?
Her kindness and love, unmeasured, so deep;
She held my hand firmly to cross the street,
She kissed me goodbye as I went to school,
Taught me God's Word, and the Golden rule.
How long, how long must I lean on Mommy?

It is time I stood up, made a plan,
It is time for me to understand,
Make her proud as I accomplish my goals,
Search for happiness and joy untold,
Make her eyes sparkle when I dedicate my life
To accept God's Word, live for Jesus Christ.
Know that He promised to make my pathway bright
If I follow the path God planned for me
To fulfill God's will for my life, my destiny.

It is time for Mommy to know,
Though her gait is measured and slow,
That I gave my life fully
To follow Jesus Christ only,
To read and to study God's Word,
To tell her that Jesus is my Lord.

Esther Schultz Connor

I reach out and take her hand,
Say, "Mommy, I do understand
To live is Christ, to die is gain;
I live by the teachings you made so plain.
Lean on me, Mommy, let's go."

I Am Accepted

To be accepted in the Godhead,
To be accepted and set free.
I am accepted and delivered
From Satan's hold, Christ died for me.

To be accepted, love was the reason.
To be accepted and redeemed.
I am accepted, God's grace and mercy
Was freely given, Christ died for me.

To be accepted in the Godhead
God Himself planned this to be.
He reached from heaven to earth and rescued
As sinner like me to join the family.

The way to redemption Christ opened,
Dying on the cross, Jesus took my place;
In love gave me the gift of righteousness.
I am saved and accepted by His grace.

Now free to enter God's presence boldly
From sinner to saint, I have been redeemed.
Free to worship, I have been accepted;
Jesus, my Savior, has won me the victory.

Esther Schultz Connor

I Speak, My Way

I use my sisters' voices
To tell you what I need.
My mother, she understands
Exactly how I feel.
From birth to my present age
Their love for me is real.
I speak, listen, hear what they say;
They gladly speak for me.

My heart speaks loud and clear,
My smile, distant, appears.
Please know I love you dearly,
Listen, hear what I say.
I look you in the eye,
You reach and take my hand;
Please speak for me, tell everyone
How thankful and blessed I am.

I daily thank my God
For the family He gave to me.
Your gentleness, your patience
True love, each day I see.
I want to shout, "I thank you!"
To each one, every day.
My sounds I make are words unsaid;
Receive my love, my way.

I Stand Therefore

EPHESIANS 6:14

I stand my head erect
Clothed in His righteousness.
No fear allowed to stay;
Truth encircles my loins each day.
My hands outstretched
Sword held in readiness,
Surrounded by an Angel band,
Secure in Jesus Christ, I stand.

I fight not with flesh and blood;
I'm a child of the Most High God.
The Holy Spirit lives within me,
The powers of darkness I can feel.
Spiritual hosts, dark powers in the heavenlies,
World rulers, wickedness, principalities;
Surrounded by an Angel band,
I wear the whole armor of God and stand.

The fight is not my own:
I stand in Christ alone.
Mercy and truth have met,
Peace exchanged a kiss with righteousness,
Satanic demons are held at bay;
Thus far and no further, Jesus Christ made it clear.
Surrounded by an Angel band,
Wearing the whole armor of God, I stand.

Esther Schultz Connor

I Will Laugh Again

Tears pool in my eyes,
I blink them back.
I will not cry.
This world of sorrow,
This world of grief,
I raise my hands to heaven,
I scream, "Is there no relief?"

The unanswered questions
Taunt me, as I try to reason why,
When God's gentle voice replies,
Whispers softly, deep inside:
"Go ahead, just cry, just cry;
Your tears I collect
In my bottle, with your name.
I see your tears,
Gently wipe them away."

"Who told you?" I asked.
"Your foreparents long ago;
Their answers tumbled
This world into woe.
I knew the future.
I knew you then;
I knew my children
Would be asking when
Will this world of sorrow and of grief
Be cleansed, renewed;
My children find relief."

Esther Schultz Connor

"Trust me, beloved offspring,
I have the power to heal,
To cleanse forever.
Satan must and will kneel.
The instigator, usurper, fiend, denied
Will be cast alive into hell by his heels
With his unholy Pride.
Laugh and rejoice, my children,
Dance around with glee,
Live holy, trust boldly,
Praise and worship ME."

I Am Delighted with You, God

I'm delighted with you, God;
Your love soothes my weary soul.
When temptations come my way,
The Holy Spirit helps me control
The urges surging deep inside,
Trying to upset my life's dreams and goals.
You surround me with your peace.
I'm a new creature, now made whole.

I no longer face each day,
Taking each moment on a whim.
I follow Jesus; He leads my way,
For I now belong to Him.
The joy I feel deep down inside,
The grace that is greater than my sin.
Come what may, whatever I face,
Cannot compare with the hope within.

I'm delighted with you, God,
Your plans for me, you have made clear.
To do your will is my delight,
To please you whether far or near.
Your mercy streams flow deep and wide;
So many trials, so many tears,
I plunge into mercy's cleansing tide,
Fully redeemed, in His presence amazed.

Esther Schultz Connor

If It Is Not One Thing

"If it is not one thing,"
I heard the old folks say.
It will be something else.
Rejoice now why you can.
Trials are waiting, and new tests;
It seems that life's pursuits,
Your visions and your dreams
 One day can turn to failure,
Upset by Satan's schemes.

Before you faint and lose heart,
Remember what Jesus said.
Satan is the god of this world,
But when you face a test,
After one thing will come another.
How much more trouble can you take?
Jesus said to be of good cheer;
He has overcome the world for your sake.

Be still and trust God's Word,
No evil that comes your way.
Will overcome your life,
God will have the final say.
He has angels standing by
To bear you up when you fall.
If it is not one thing, it is something else,
God promised victory; trust Him, that is all.

In God's Time

Lucifer the Angel, brilliant Morningstar above
Was warped and twisted, hating the people God so loved.
Demonic deity, craving power, wanting to take God's place,
Brought evil into the world,
Affecting the whole human race.
Mankind was hopeless, seemed all was lost.
We failed miserably each day,
Even though we knew sin's deadly cost.

The answer was Jesus Christ, God's beloved Son.
God's Word tells us how it was and will be done;
It will happen one day, in God's own time.

Some blame God for all their problems,
They feel that He is the one to blame.
They want God to put an end to suffering now,
To heal all the sick and the lame.
God in His mercy and grace had planned,
Even before this world began,
To cleanse the world from sin
That has affected every man.

The answer still is Jesus Christ God's beloved Son.
God's Word tells us how it was and will be done;
It will happen one day, in God's own time.

God knew our weakness; there is no doubt
Such love, no one can figure it out.
But just receive gladly, God himself made a way.
Accept righteousness God extends, a free gift today;

Esther Schultz Connor

Only those who receive Jesus Christ as Savior and Lord
Can enter heaven, that holy place, salvation's reward.
No sin can enter heaven, God's Word makes it plain.
In God's time, His children will enjoy Paradise regained.

The answer still is Jesus Christ God's beloved Son.
God's Word tells us how it was and will be done;
It will happen one day, in God's own time.

In You I Abide

I love how you call me beloved
As you reach out and take my hand.
I can trust you where my trace ends;
I know you will understand.
You hear my thoughts unspoken,
You answer when I pray.
My heart loves to hear you whisper;
You are with me all the way.

I don't have to wait until our lives end
For you to wipe away all my tears.
You hold me when I am lonesome.
You whisper, "Have no fear."
You give me your sweet assurance,
Nothing can come between our love.
You will be with me now and forever,
You will take me home above.

Sweet mystery, your divine love
Has no distance, will never end.
I enjoy this peace of knowing
You call me child and friend.
Father God, Jesus my Savior,
Holy Spirit, Comforter, and Guide
I have all I need or imagine
Life abundant, in you I abide.

Esther Schultz Connor

Irreversibly Blessed

God does not lie,
The Word confirms it:
He means just what He says.
His Words, His promises
Says truly, we are irreversibly blessed.
Whatever God says determines
No one can deny or reverse it.
God is not a man,
He is the great I am.
What God has blessed stays blessed.

We are irreversibly blessed.
No one can change or reverse it
For come what may, God's final say
Is His children once blessed, shall stay
Completely, irreversibly blessed.

From Abraham to Jesus the Lamb
Men have trusted in God's Word.
Many went astray,
False gods they claimed
Instead of God whose love had earned it.
Men schemed and lied,
Suffered and died,
But God His Word had spoken
To those who believed
On Jesus Christ
And forgiveness received,
Deliverance and blessings followed.

Esther Schultz Connor

We are irreversibly blessed.
No one can change or reverse it.
For come what may, God's final say
Is His children once blessed, shall stay
Completely, irreversibly blessed.

It Is All About Him

The blood of Jesus God's Son
Cleanses us from all sin.
We thank Him for all that He's done,
Opened heaven's door, let us in.

It is all about Him.
"Thank you, Jesus,"
I am praising. I am praising Him;
His name is so sweet,
I have to repeat,
"Thank you, Jesus,"
It is all about Him.

Now I am saved by His grace,
No more bound in sin.
I swiftly run life's race
A crown of life I did win.

O friend, don't you see,
It was done for me and you
Jesus hung on that tree,
Paid our price that was due.

It is all about Him.
"Thank you, Jesus,"
I am praising. I am praising Him;
His name is so sweet,
I have to repeat,
"Thank you, Jesus,"
It is all about Him.

Esther Schultz Connor

It Is All About You, God

You blessed me with life, oh so wonderful.
You infilled me with your divine breath.
You did not call me barren, nor childless,
You gave me children; I am so blessed.

You called me chosen, adopted by your name.
You knew me before the foundation of the world.
You were not surprised when I came to life.
You were the author, the finisher, by faith I learned.

You never left my side, even when I went astray.
You knew where I wandered and roamed.
You sought me, like the Good Shepherd you cared,
You left the ninety-nine, helped me find my way home.

You opened the door each time I appeared;
You welcomed me back with your sweet, gentle smile.
You touched my heart and healed my wounds,
You whispered, "lay down and rest for a while."

You created a beautiful world, uncharted universe.
You gave me eyes to see all that you made.
You celebrated my battles won, victorious pursuits.
You showed me the path of light, guided my way.

You were the unseen guest when I felt so alone,
You loved me, encouraged, and comforted my soul.
You blessed me with life everlasting, deliverance from sin's hold.
You deserve my praise, my worship, to obey you is my goal.

Joy Comes

JOHN 16:22

You now, therefore, have sorrow
Is what Jesus said.
He will see us again,
He will see us again,
Then our hearts will rejoice.
We'll throw away our sorrow,
For tomorrow,
Joy comes tomorrow.

Such joy when we see Jesus,
As He said,
No one can take our joy,
No one can take our joy;
The joy of the Lord
It is our strength.
For tomorrow,
Joy comes tomorrow.

Joy conquers sorrow.
Such joy in Jesus,
When we see Jesus,
When we see Jesus,
Our hearts will rejoice.
We'll throw away our sorrow.
Joy conquers sorrow;
Joy comes today and tomorrow.

Esther Schultz Connor

Just Like Me

Look at me;
What do you see?
A mirror reflection
Of what God made me to be.
You make an assumption,
You decide you are right.
Just what do you think
May be only a shadow of the light.

I sit in the chair by my bedside quietly,
My hands folded in my lap.
I stare blankly ahead at times,
Sometimes smiling at what I see.
No response most times to your questions,
I hum to myself a song.
You lean in to listen closer,
That tune lingers in your mind all day long.

You look at me,
But cannot see
The person deep within.
I once was young,
But now I am old;
So much living comes between.
The dash between birth and death,
A long life's journey I have seen.

I smile as I remember
The person I used to be.
I laughed, I sang,

Enjoying the audience's energy,
Encore they shouted to me.
A few curtain calls,
Signed some autographs,
The love they gave to me.
The nectar of performance,
The thrill of victory,
Meant so much then to me.

Look at me again,
Gaze deeply into my eyes.
Can you see the person God meant to be?
Not your mind concocted lies.
The shell before you that you see
May seem so very far away
From the man, the woman, you will be
When I've left here and gone home to stay
To where forever I will be.

I am your future,
You will look just like me.
One day another will be trying to see
As you sit quietly and stare.
You may smile or even speak,
Your voice a thread, a whisper
Of what it used to be.
So, grant me some indulgence,
Be kind as you can be.
One day the great exchange will be made,
And you will become just like me.

The difference between us,
Please listen closely,
Is the place that I will be
With Jesus, friends, and loved ones,
In that Royal family,

Esther Schultz Connor

In the book of life, your name must be written.
Like the true believers up above,
Filled with God's peace and love.
In those mansions, Christ promised
To prepare in heaven for one just like me.

God's mercy He pours,
Freely given, it is yours.
Accept, believe and receive
The free gift of righteousness and peace.
Sin unforgiven is a death sentence you see,
You will be found guilty, hell-bound.
Darkness, sorrow, no defense
For those who refuse to repent; O soul be found.
Complete in Jesus Christ, heaven-bound,
New life, eternity awaits, for one just like me.

Just Trust Him

Just place your trust in God
Jesus the Savior as your Lord.
In sorrow or in pain,
Just lean upon His Word.
When your heart is overwhelmed
At times you just don't know;
Let Jesus take the helm
He knows which way to go.

When your heart is filled with pain
With tears and there's no relief,
God's Word makes it plain,
Cast your cares on Christ, believe.
He knows the path to take,
Leave all in His control.
Whether sleeping or awake,
In His hands, He has your soul.

So, walk with Him in faith,
He loves you more than you can know.
Keep running your life's race,
Hold on to Jesus, and don't let go.
God's promised to hear your prayers.
He'll answer when you call.
Just trust Him and obey
The victory is yours.

Esther Schultz Connor

Kingdom Ready

I live in peace with God my Father,
Secured by Christ Jesus, the Son.
The covenant is real,
My future is sealed.
I stand victorious; the victory's won.

God's design was settled, delivered,
When Jesus said, "It is finished," and died.
My sin debt was paid,
His righteousness He gave.
I'm forgiven, set free, justified.

Now I walk life's uncertain pathways.
The joy that is mine, through Christ freely given,
No matter what comes.
God's will be done
In my life and in yours, as in heaven.

God desires that all of His creation
Trust in Jesus, on Him believe.
The last days are here,
No one will be spared,
Only those who forgiveness receive.

Now God's our Father in heaven
We hallow His name, His love divine,
Forgiving as forgiven.
A new life in Jesus we're living;
Redeemed, kingdom ready, we shine.

Last Forever and Endure

Seems like it was only yesterday
As a little girl, I sang and played.
In the garden among flowers multi-hued,
I ran around, believing
That a childhood so delightful
Days like these would last forever and endure.

Oh, the sweet sounds of children laughing,
As they dance and play while passing.
I smile and reminisce for just a while;
Childhood days last but a moment,
Elude one's grasp as we try to hold them.
Days like these don't last forever or endure.

Let the children play with laughter,
Enjoy the good times and their chatter.
Let's not rob them of what we call the good old days;
This is their time to enjoy them,
To build their memories for all time,
Fleeting moments to last forever and endure.

God, our Heavenly Father, gives us
Days of peace, hope, laughter, and enjoyment.
Jesus died, rose, gives life abundantly,
Sin and self would try to rob us
Of the pleasure that awaits those
Who believe, receive love that lasts forever and endures.

Esther Schultz Connor

Life's Rhythms and Flow

Another week, another day,
Another moment, to give you praise.
You know my name, call me your own.
You are the strength I lean upon.
You are the author and finisher of my faith,
The road on which I travel,
The path my destiny takes.

At times I struggle and feel alone,
The road is narrow; many friends are gone.
The peace within, the joy I feel
Comes from the Holy Spirit, I am sealed.
Troubles assail, without, within,
The devil smiles, satanic grins.
Does he not know his doom is sure?
I'm of royal blood; Jesus Christ is my Lord.

Another week, another day,
Another moment, to give you praise.
Come what may, although times are grim,
I will praise my Savior, rely on Him.
The times and tides are in His control:
My life, my being, my very soul,
My heart's delight, my Lord, my King,
My joy, my future, my everything.

Linger in God's Presence

The strength you need
To face each day,
The courage to handle
Whatever comes your way.
Life's uncertain moments
Can cause fear and dismay.
Let God's presence begin your day.

Delight and cherish God's holy presence,
Your heart needs the strength of His Word.
Enter with singing, praises you bring Him;
Linger, learn in the presence of the holy Lord.

The mind, it may wander
Thoughts run to and fro,
Trying to distract you from God's holy glow.
Stand firm or prostrate fall,
Shout hallelujahs to the Holy LORD.
God is waiting, anticipating
For you to linger in His holy presence.

The Holy Spirit waits, a gentle breeze
Wafts God's goodness fills your needs.
Lift your hands high, the joyful cup to fill.
God is gracious, it is His will.
He gives you the strength to help you on your way,
So, linger and be renewed in His presence every day.

Esther Schultz Connor

Delight and cherish God's holy presence,
Your heart needs the strength of His Word.
Enter with singing, praises you bring Him;
Linger, learn in the presence of the holy Lord.

Listen:
God's Creation Speaks

PSALM 121

Creation shows forth God's glory,
The hills and mountains, they echo His praise.
Mysterious and inscrutable they stand.
Listen, they speak of the Ancient of Days.
He loves and cares for you, His child beloved;
He is on your side, now and forevermore.
He called your name, knew your life's story
Before the day that you were born.

As far as your eyes can see, the mountains
And the distant hills they beckon you,
Listen closely; they seem to say,
"Lift up your eyes and look our way!
God the Almighty Creator and Lord
Who made the heavens and the earth
Shows forth His glory, the heavens display
To remind you His beloved child, each day
Of his power to save, keep all evil away."

Listen closely as the hills and mountains speak.
They seem to touch your heart and soul,
They are a sight wondrous to behold.
Mysterious and inscrutable they stand.
To say, reach for God's outstretched hands.
You're never alone; His watchful eyes keep
You in His sight, both night and day;

Esther Schultz Connor

He never slumbers, nor does He sleep,
He's your help, your keeper, your rock, your mainstay.

God keeps your feet strong, provides the shade
When the sun shines brightly all the day.
The moon's soft, gentle glow at night
Reminds you that you are precious in His sight.
When doubt and fears try to oppress your soul,
Look up; the Lord reminds you, He's in total control.
He knows when you go out or enter in.
He preserves your life; remember, you belong to Him.

Make It Christmas Every Day

Christmas is a word so special and real,
Peace, love, and harmony are what we feel.
Christmas began from the moment of Jesus' birth
Brought hope alive, to all creation, mankind, on earth
To people everywhere, little boys and girls,
To the men and women, over the entire world.

Won't it be wonderful to have Christmas every day?
For everyone to make it real, to mean what we say,
To look each other straight in the eyes,
To give love, live in peace, forget the lies,
To make it real, help others along the way;
Make it Christmas, each and every day.

The smile, the greetings, from people we meet
Strangers with goodwill, now we greet;
Peace, love and harmony, everywhere,
Children playing together in the village square.
Christmas makes the difference we need, that is clear;
The sounds of Christmas love changes the atmosphere.

Let us decide to have Christmas every day,
Heed the call everyone, let us start today.
The men, women, children, we see everywhere
Reflect God's image, the choice is clear.
Let peace, love and harmony be displayed,
Becoming our future, let us make it Christmas every day.

Esther Schultz Connor

Meet Jesus in the Air

When the trumpet sounds and Jesus returns,
We'll rise and meet Him in the air.
How wonderful to see precious loved ones
And families so dear.
Oh friend, get ready now,
There's no time for delay.
Prepare to go, eternal joy you'll know,
We'll rise and meet Jesus in the air.

Get ready now to meet Him,
To meet Him in the air.
When the trumpet sounds,
We'll leave the ground,
There's no time for delay.
Just give your heart to Jesus;
He's calling out your name.
Get ready now to meet Him,
To meet King Jesus in the air.

So precious friends and loved ones,
You have no time to waste.
You may be called at any moment,
So, hurry, don't delay.
Make ready now, prepare your heart,
Christ is calling out your name.
He loves you so; I hope you know
Joy unspeakable, divine love awaits.

More Precious Than Silver or Gold

What will you give in exchange for your soul?
Your search for happiness, in wealth untold.
Money brings temporary pleasure, a smile on your face,
That fades and diminishes, for it's only a taste.

Then power, career, they call your name;
Oh, what a successful life you've attained!
You give your orders, left and right,
Your goals, ambitions, your deals, and delights.

The question still remains for you:
What can compare to all that you do?
Your soul is precious even more than gold,
Than fame, success, and wealth untold.

The rich man so wealthy in hell opened his eyes;
What a horrible place, a deadly surprise,
Nothing else mattered; his dreams, they were shattered.
His soul was more precious than silver or gold.

So, give your life to the great I am,
The Savior Jesus Christ, God's risen lamb.
The price He paid, your soul to save
Is so much more precious than wealth's display.

Esther Schultz Connor

My Flesh Is Weak

Oh Lord, I'm so tired!
My stubborn will, my way,
The debt of sin's desire,
The price I surely must pay.
No fleeting moments of pleasure
Can ever take the place.
I realize deep inside, I can't rely
On Satan's lying guarantee,
Empty promises he made.

My flesh at times so weak,
Found it so hard to refuse
The things my body craved,
The evil Satanic lures.
Though pleasing and tempting,
At times to my foolish taste
Like bitter gall, earned my despair,
Such a sorry, shameful waste.
"O wretched man," the psalmist cried,
"Who delivers me from this body that lied?"

God is the answer to the question we seek,
He reaches out His hands in mercy and love
To rescue the worn, the weary, and the weak;
That's why He sent Jesus from heaven above.
I'm not alone, I must confess,
God seeks my good and nothing less;
No mishap too great, no problem too small.
God loves and cares; He knows it all.

Esther Schultz Connor

If I would seek Him, as Savior and friend,
He'll walk beside me to life's end.

I need your help, Lord,
Your power and grace divine.
Come touch and strengthen
This weary heart of mine.
My life and times, Lord Jesus,
I place in your nail-pierced hands.
My flesh must submit and not question
But follow your holy demands.
I yield my life to your control
My will, my body, my weary soul;
I lean my head in your embrace.
Holy Spirit, live within me,
Help me to run this race.

My Loved One Died

My disappointment is real.
I must reveal,
I never expected things to end this way.
I stood on God's Word,
Prayed daily for the Lord
To deliver and heal without delay.

As each day went by
Till my loved one died.
I wondered where I had failed,
Then I heard a voice deep down inside,
"It's not for you to say
What month or what day,
Or whom I will take home to stay."

"You do not realize
Why your loved one died.
How sometimes pain and sickness
Come into play.
I am God of the past, present, and future, my child,
And I determine the end of the day."

"It is hard for you to see
How much my people mean to me.
I created each one for my very own;
I love them much more
Than you can ever know.
Trust me, my child,
It's my loved one that died."

Esther Schultz Connor

Think of this while you cry;
My Son Jesus shouted, "It is finished," and died.
You weep, and you do not weep alone;
I understand how you feel,
Your pain as you grieve,
That's why one day, sorrow and death will be finally gone.

My Mother's God

When I was young,
I served faithfully
The God of my mother;
Her faith lifted me.
I felt sweet assurance
Whenever Mom was near.
Her prayers lifted me upwards;
I felt so spiritual when mother prayed.

The years flew by swiftly,
My life was my own.
I missed my Mother's prayers,
I was an adult all alone.
The foundation Mom planted
Helped me to decide
To continue to follow
The Lord as my guide.

I fell in love with sweet Jesus,
Our relationship had changed.
I prayed on a personal level,
Not only through my mother's prayers.
At times we still prayed together,
Then my mother's prayers and my own,
Ascended up to heaven's throne,
To my God and not my mother's God alone.

Now I pray for my own dear children,
I encourage them strongly, too,
To seek God and to serve Him,

Esther Schultz Connor

As I continued to do.
I had relied on my mother's prayers,
But soon the time came (as would theirs)
When my mother's God became my God;
The relationship had to change.

My Tears

My pain at times is a comfort;
I hold my pain close to my heart,
When I have no words to describe it;
Hot tears from my eyes do start.
My tears ease the sharp sting of sorrow,
A soothing balm for distress and grief.
I'm reminded of Jesus' tears also,
Just before Lazarus from the dead, He raised.

He feels my distress, knows my weakness;
He holds me close, soothes my deepest despair.
My tears remind me: Jesus promises
One day to take sorrow, pain, and tears away.

I thank God in all of His wisdom,
He provides tears as an outlet for grief.
As stiff upper lip, some have chosen
As their way to find some relief.
Tears are like raindrops from heaven,
Bringing life to dry thirsty soil.
So, let your tears flow,
For one day, you know,
Sorrow, pain, death, and tears will be gone.

He feels my distress, knows my weakness;
He holds me close, soothes my deepest despair.
My tears remind me: Jesus promises
One day to take sorrow, pain, and tears away.

Esther Schultz Connor

My True Journey Has Just Begun

Do not weep for me, my loved ones,
You know it says in God's Word
That when a believer leaves this earth,
He begins forever in heaven with the Lord.

The transition is oh so painless;
Absent from the body, I go
To join precious loved ones and family
Who left here some time ago.

You look at the shell of my spirit,
The broken flesh that I once called home.
I am no longer there. I have departed;
At last, my true journey has begun.

The welcome I know that awaits me
Is a celebration I can hardly wait.
As Angels escort me to heaven,
I pass through the eastern gates

The wonders I gaze on, the splendor,
I could never imagine it would be so.
I look down and then realize it
I am walking, how I just don't know.

Esther Schultz Connor

I see faces of saints now departed,
My loved ones and family are there.
I join in the glad celebration,
Praise and worship filled the atmosphere.

Now I see King Jesus in His majestic glory,
The Savior, the Lamb who died for me.
I fell to my knees and cried, "Holy!
Thank you, God, oh how I love thee."

The earth that we live and inhabit
Is only a temporary home.
Our true dwelling is in heaven;
My true journey has only just begun.

No Good Thing

PSALM 34

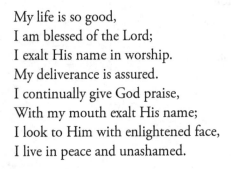

My life is so good,
I am blessed of the Lord;
I exalt His name in worship.
My deliverance is assured.
I continually give God praise,
With my mouth exalt His name;
I look to Him with enlightened face,
I live in peace and unashamed.

I sought the Lord,
He heard my cry;
From fear delivered me.
To those desiring life
God invites to taste and see.
Of His goodness, I will boast
And magnify His name.
His eyes are fixed on me;
My trust in Him will never change.

No want or need appears,
No hunger God will not fill.
The righteous cry and He hears
Those who desire to do His will.
He is near to the broken heart,
And the contrite spirit He will save.
To those that seek the Lord
No good thing will He not let them have.

Esther Schultz Connor

No Longer a Mystery

I am breathless,
I am hopeful,
I trust in God.
My cup is so full
Of joy, love, and peace;
I was born to live forever,
I was born to inhabit eternity.

I see my face in the mirror
And it's a wondrous mystery to me.
Who is that looking back at me?
Furrowed brow, destined to be free,
Born to think, to love, to be brave,
To trust in God, come what may.

Longing to see in this life's race,
A smile of pride on God my heavenly Father's face
As He smiles and boasts
To the heavenly hosts,
"There, don't you see,
One who wants to be
Just like Me,
My precious child, victorious and free,
To inhabit a new universe, a destiny."

The Word of God tells me clearly
This is definitely not a dream.
My faith's substance is seen
Evidence of the unseen.

Esther Schultz Connor

I was born to live forever,
I was born to inhabit eternity;
That is no longer a mystery to me.

No Matter What

I am trusting God no matter what,
No matter where or what we have got.
Our God is Lord, the ruler of all;
I trust Him with my life, my all.

When life seems to turn upside down,
I still wear a smile; no need to frown.
My God, Deliverer, Redeemer, Friend
Knows the beginning and the end.

So, no matter what, I stand erect;
Though pressures come, my faith is tested.
Tried sometimes beyond what I can bear,
The mighty God, He's always there.

I trust in Him; I lift high my hands
To praise my God, the great I am.
My God, I love Him; words cannot describe
The joy I feel when I am close to His side.

God deserves my worship and my praise;
I lift my voice, sweet notes I will raise
To celebrate, hold fast to what we have got;
I trust in God, no matter what.

Esther Schultz Connor

No Patient Is Truly Alone

Reach out and take my hand,
Please know you are not alone.
I promise to stand by your side,
Be your hope, even though your strength is gone.
I see the tears that you cry,
The pain and discomfort that you feel;
I join my Healthcare Team's services,
We fight until you are healed.

So much we do not understand,
Your faces come and go;
But each one of you touches my heart,
You have a special place there, you know.
You are not just a room or a number,
I will fight for you until the end.
You return home with family
Or I bid you goodbye, my friend.

I care for you, don't you know?
I pray for you night and day
As I perform my duties of care
In my own efficient, special way.
I touch a fevered brow,
I hold an unsteady hand,
Behind my mask, I smile,
I am part of the Healthcare Band.

I stand in for family and friends,
I handle their loved ones with care;
A gentle voice, a tender touch

Esther Schultz Connor

Helps to drive gloom away.
At this moment, in each person's life,
It hurts so much more when you are alone.
I promise to be more than what you need,
I am on duty and will fight for you until the battle is won.

The Health Care Team are like Angels,
Ministering to God's creation in need.
They give of their time, from morning till night,
Broken-hearted, but performing good deeds.
Each Team Member functions in service,
Working hard, making a victory stand.
Each loss is a dagger that pierces the heart;
God bless and protect His Angel band.

I know in God's Word it is written
The plans that God has for you and me.
The trials of life that we now face
Precedes peace, joy, and victory.
Sin entered the world; that is the reason
Mankind suffers in sickness and pain.
God sent Jesus Christ, a perfect sacrifice,
To restore us to new life, forever with Him.

Not Guilty

I stood a helpless victim,
Filled with fear and despair.
Life had tossed me this way and that way,
Hopeless, discouraged; no one seemed to care.

The jury had considered,
Their determination was clear.
I knew that I was guilty,
No defense could prevail.

I tried once, twice, faltered,
I could not deny.
My past overwhelmed me,
God help me, I cried.

The Judge of all the ages,
God the Father, holy and just,
I looked left, right and center;
Was there anyone left for me to trust?

When with light streams of glory,
His vesture dipped in blood.
"Release him, not guilty,"
Said the Holy Son of God.

"His sins are forgiven;
That is why I hung on the cross.
The robe that he is now wearing
Says he is righteous, not lost."

Esther Schultz Connor

The Angels were singing,
I joined in with glee.
Hallelujah, thank you, Jesus!
Your grace and mercy set me free.

Now I am free to trust in Jesus,
To follow and obey.
He died, rose victorious,
My heavenly mansion is prepared.

I have a new life, filled with promise,
My joy is on display.
I love Jesus Christ, my Redeemer;
The Holy Spirit leads my way.

Not Unto Us, O Lord

PSALM 115

Not unto us O Lord,
But unto Your holy name.
You deserve all our praise,
You are every day the same.

Our pride may lift us high,
Our idols we justify;
Your mercy and truth cannot be denied,
Your name we must glorify.

You, God, inhabit the heavens,
You, God, inhabit our praise.
You do whatsoever pleases you,
You help both small and great.

Our children, you promise to bless,
To increase us more and more;
Not unto us O Lord, in You we trust,
We bless your name now and forevermore.

Esther Schultz Connor

One Family in the Faith

One body, one faith, one baptism, one Lord,
One hope found in Jesus, a love that endures.
Peace passing understanding, by faith secured,
A new home in heaven, a mansion, a blessed reward.

All our friends and loved ones, accepting Jesus will be there;
God created a family a world of no cares.
Come on into this family,
The redeemed by Christ's blood divine,
One family in the faith God says, "these are mine."

All those who surrender, accepting God's grace,
Freely given, His mercy, our sin debts erased.
God-given gifts of hope, freedom no one can destroy,
Such serene contentment, hearts renewed, and joy.

Satisfaction guaranteed, His blessings abound,
Poured out unmeasured, through faith in Jesus is found.
Come on into this family, the redeemed by Christ's blood divine,
One family in the faith God says, "these are mine."

Perfected Forever

HEBREWS 10:14

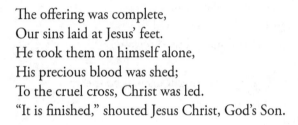

The offering was complete,
Our sins laid at Jesus' feet.
He took them on himself alone,
His precious blood was shed;
To the cruel cross, Christ was led.
"It is finished," shouted Jesus Christ, God's Son.

His grace He gave so freely,
I did not deserve such mercy.
God's beloved Son, for sin, was on display;
The earth, it groaned and shuddered,
Graves opened up, it thundered;
Something strange was happening that day.

The sun refused to shine,
Darkness stepped out of time,
The entrance to the holiest had begun,
The temple veil was torn
From the top to the bottom;
God was glorified when some saw what was done.

Jesus the only way to God most holy;
Now I enter God's presence boldly.
Jesus suffered, died, and took my place,
Now I am free to enter in,
A child of God, set free from sin,
Not a sinner, or a beggar, in disgrace.

Esther Schultz Connor

That one offering was complete,
Forever perfected, God was pleased.
Jesus' sacrifice brought victory for me,
A new life, full and sweet.
God redeemed and set me free,
Set apart to love and serve Him faithfully.

Saturate Yourself in His Love

God's love is indescribable,
It's honey-sweet to my taste.
The flow is undeniable,
My whole being is amazed.
God pours His love like lava,
Flowing through my senses, my soul.
It is mystical,
It is supernatural,
It is glorious from head to toe.

The one who accepts and experiences
This love, this glory divine,
Feels satisfied and enraptured
To know, to taste this heavenly wine.
To enter God's presence boldly
Is the right of every believer.
It is amazing,
It is delightful,
It is a free gift; become a love receiver.

Reach out, all you who need such love,
Real love that is kind and true.
God's love requires no scorecard,
It is not based on what you do.
The breath you breathe is a mystery;
You live and exist by God's loving plan.

Esther Schultz Connor

It is exciting,
It is at times overwhelming;
Saturate yourself in God's love for man.

Science and God's Word

Positive emotions, peace, and goodwill
Leave feelings of happiness, hope, dreams fulfilled.
Gratitude, thanksgiving, they quickly take the place
Of negative thoughts, emotions that leave a bitter taste.

Science and God's Word both agree,
Stress takes a toll, a role quite deadly.
Brainstem releases hormones; you can choose
A victorious path, to win or lose.

God's Word reminds us to give our lives to prayer,
Give thanks to God for everything, everywhere;
Focus on happiness, joy-filled dreams,
Rewire your brain, enhance self-esteem.

The joy of the Lord, it gives you strength,
Protects your heart's inner defense;
Elated moods, that gloom erases,
Excitement builds, gratitude anticipates.

Defeat negative thoughts, give them no yielding;
It's up to you, stress can be defeated.
Be thankful, enjoy every moment you live,
Give love, give thanks to God, be positive, forgive.

Science follows God's Word; it is true;
Live well, show kindness in all that you do.
Enhance the positive, defeat the negative, in your life everyday,
Be joyful, excited, delighted; stress relief is here to stay.

Esther Schultz Connor

Science is amazing; yet more to understand and discover;
In God's Word, His will for mankind is clear, from cover to cover.
Jesus said, "I am the way the truth and the life, you see;
No one comes to the Father, except through Me."

Stress Relief

Stress takes you on a journey
You do not want to go.
It can bring you pain and heartache,
Anxiety, depression, and woe,
Upsets the balance of wellness.
You worry about what cannot be done;
You need stress relief
Before your doom is sealed
And stress celebrates it has won.

The scientific research tells us
The steps we need to take.
It takes a sweet, loving, forgiving spirit,
A thankful heart; make no mistake,
God's Word gives us His promise;
He will help you, it can be done.
Give your life to Jesus Christ
The battle is over, the victory He won.

The first step is, be reconciled to God.
He loves you so; you know,
He sent Jesus Christ to die for your sins.
In this world of sorrow, sickness, and woe,
Follow the path that stress relief requires.
Give your burdens to Jesus; that is His desire.
Why worry, why stress,
Revel in God's goodness,
God's love, grace, and mercy will relieve all your stress.

Esther Schultz Connor

Tears Don't Win

In the depths of my heart and soul,
Tear filled ducts stand ready to roll;
Secured by will and fortitude, they stand in place.
I wish sometimes I could cry and the pain erase,
But I stand firm though a few tears may escape.
I hold them in firmly in check, with an attitude of grace;
Why cry, with hot tears falling down your cheeks?
Why cry and divulge to others such pain and misery?
I wait instead patiently for the wonderful day
When God promises to wipe all tears away.

Till then, I stand firm, head held high,
Chin tilted upwards, looking you in the eye;
Jesus, my Savior, gave His life in my place,
My debt of sin canceled, all is erased.
I am free to walk life's highway
From beginning to the end.
Jesus Christ is with me; on Him I always depend.
So, no matter what befalls me, tomorrow or today,
No matter endless misery, no matter what people say,
I am determined to smile often, tears held at bay;
Focus on each blessed moment, and celebrate, come what may.

Thanks for the Memories

So many thoughts of days present, and those gone by,
Memories so special, they moisten my eyes.
God, you've been a friend, tried, tested and true,
Amazing and special, you do the things that you do.
I trusted you then, such a long time ago
I know you were with me in joy, sorrow, and woe.

You showed me your presence; you made that so clear
From my earliest memories, I knew you were there.
Endearing your presence, to me you revealed;
Even a child can distinguish and know that they are sealed.
The miracles of healing, protection from danger, foolish decisions made;
You were my help, my comfort through the childhood patterns laid.

Memories are so special, that day we recognized
The God of creation as Father, Jesus Christ, was once himself a child,
The stories of Jesus began to make life's reasons so clear,
The world we hold dearly will one day disappear,
Then the Kingdom of heaven will descend like a bride adorned;
With joy and celebration, a new earth will be found.

God himself made the changes from beginning to end,
From the first, dark and formless, the Holy Spirit hovered to amend.
A beautiful heaven and earth, God Himself did prepare
For mankind to live in, a wonderful world to inhabit and share.
Scenes of beauty and treasures, animals free, not wild,
No wilderness of thorns, no dangers lurking, defiled,
Until the destroyer wicked Satan, his doom he'd received,
His slick words of knowledge the woman deceived.

Esther Schultz Connor

God knew the end from the beginning; it's true,
Free will and man's choice would reveal what we knew.
Jesus died on the cruel cross, paid that awesome price
To lead the children back to the Father, the redeemed born twice.
All these thoughts bathed in love streams of glory divine
Forever leave their imprints on this heart of mine.
Thank you, God my heavenly Father; I can hardly comprehend
The wonderful memories of you, the Holy Spirit, Jesus my Savior and friend.

The Debt Was Paid

I know that you love me dearly,
I know that you really care.
You surround me with your presence,
So with you, I have no fear.
The Holy Spirit indwells and leads me
All along the paths I take.
Your divine assurance, your eyes upon me
Keep me centered every day.

I know, there's no doubt, I'm settled,
No anxious feelings can destroy
The faith on which I stand boldly,
Your presence brings unspeakable joy.
I'll sing and shout your praises,
My flesh must yield, your will I'll obey;
The Holy Spirit bears the sweetest witness.
I am yours; the debt's been paid

Glory to your name, dear Savior,
You took all my sin and shame;
When you died, a sinner sentenced
For a debt mankind could not pay.
You rose the third day, triumphant, glorious,
Your sacrifice, it set me free.
The stripes upon your back, dear Lord Jesus,
Brought healing and victory for me.

God's love, it has no limits,
His grace abounds to me.
When Jesus shouted, "it is finished,"

Esther Schultz Connor

That sealed the covenant, set me free.
My name is written down in heaven,
In the book of life, the Holy Spirit reveals.
I'm in the family of the chosen
Believers blood-bought and redeemed.

The Eyes of My Heart

The eyes of my heart see the invisible;
The things that bring fear and dismay
Are only phantoms, shadows that surround me,
They disappear in the light of day.

I see the news, distress and panic,
Fear of falling, gloom, and despair;
The eyes of my heart see God's deliverance,
Angel armies surround Satan's array.

God knows the end from the beginning,
His truth and mercy will forever stand.
My heart's eyes focus shifts from earth to glory,
Piercing the darkness to see the Angel band.

God's grace is sufficient, meets my every need;
His promises, reassurance say, "peace be still."
My help and deliverance come from God above,
I lift the eyes of my heart up to see glory's hills.

Esther Schultz Connor

The Fragrance of Hope

Hope is the fragrance of tomorrow,
The evidence of things not yet seen.
Today there's no need for me to borrow,
Reaching out to grab from tomorrow's theme.

Hope's fragrance fills the atmosphere
Through many a dark, gloomy day.
The answer God sends from His garden;
Blooms of hope, joy and peace light my way.

So, hope streams a light in the darkness,
I reach out with an unsteady hand;
The Holy Spirit's inner witness
Reminds me that God's in holy command.

Hope's fragrance revives my soul, delivers a promise;
On God's Word, I can truly rely.
The truth to my heart revealed is:
God loves me; hope's fragrance will never die.

The Last Enemy

That phone call late at night
Or any hour of the day
Shatters your heart in a million pieces;
You feel every atom of your clay.
Thoughts explode within your head,
Your heart shatters in disbelief.
Maybe you heard the news wrongly,
Didn't understand what was said,
Anything to delay that awful grief.

He's gone forever.
She's gone never to return.
It can't be true.
No matter what you do,
Your heart is so heavy.
This load you can't bear;
What can replace this feeling,
You've been caught unaware.

You vicious enemy,
You godless thief,
How dare you attack!
You bring no relief.
What fostered such hatred,
What feeds your wicked desire?
What did we do to cause you
To engulf our whole being in fire?

Dear God, we cry out in misery and pain;
Dear God, help us face life

Esther Schultz Connor

For just one more day;
The loss of a loved one,
We know that you care.
You had to forsake for a moment
Your beloved Son so dear.

"It is finished," Jesus cried
Upon that cruel cross.
"Death's only a shadow,
Fear no evil or loss.
Take my hand; I am with you
From beginning to end.
I'm your constant companion,
Your Savior and Friend."

The Lord Is Good

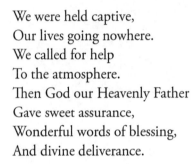

We were held captive,
Our lives going nowhere.
We called for help
To the atmosphere.
Then God our Heavenly Father
Gave sweet assurance,
Wonderful words of blessing,
And divine deliverance.

It is no dream,
Our blessing streams.
The Lord is great, The Lord is good;
Our mouths filled with laughter,
Our tongues kept on singing,
"The Lord is great, the Lord is good."

We sowed in tears and weeping,
Made long our furrows.
The heathens were happy,
We looked for better tomorrows.
Then God our Father stepped in,
They all bore witness
He made a way for His children.

Now we plant precious seed,
God's own mighty Word;
Come home with shouts of joy,
Rejoicing in the Lord.

Esther Schultz Connor

The harvest is truly ready,
The reapers called God's own.
Bring home the sheaves of plenty,
Be glad for what God's done.

It is no dream,
Our blessing streams,
The Lord is great, the Lord is good.
Our mouths filled with laughter,
Our tongues kept on singing,
"The Lord is great, the Lord is good."

The Stages of Life

A wondrous journey,
Paths given or chosen;
The stages and phases of our lives,
At times wonderful, exciting, calm, and peaceful,
At times filled with fury, hurt, and strife.
The unending pursuit
Of what we can't understand,
The whys and the wherefores,
The stages of man.

The birth and the sorrow,
The laughter and pain,
The wonderful sunshine,
The snow and the rain.
The seasons deliver
Their assigned plan;
The snow falls in winter,
The waves cover the sand.

The sunbeams at noonday,
The night's darkness begins;
Sleep comes softly on tiptoe,
Earth's rhythms within.
The mystery of life's patterns
The beginning and the end
Is really a promise,
An inscrutable friend.

Esther Schultz Connor

God knows all the answers.
Mankind's destiny reveals,
God is our lives' driver,
Move over, let Him have the wheel
His love underwrites,
Our journey displays,
The hands of the Creator,
The Ancient of days.

We're told, can't imagine
What joys lie in store
For those who choose Jesus
As Savior and Lord.
They inherit earth's boundaries,
A world renewed, undefiled,
Nature's harmonious melodies,
Creation's majestic divide.

Jesus has been preparing
Such wondrous treasures yet unseen.
Jump in fellow travelers,
Our lives we must yield;
Our thoughts and our motives,
Let God have complete control.
Joy unspeakable, unimaginable
Awaits the redeemed, resurrected soul.

Time Is Fleeting

Magical moments,
Hearts beat fast,
I look into your eyes,
The moments they last.
The sweetness of love,
That eternal flame,
Time is the essence;
I whisper your name.

The days go by swiftly,
Winter becomes spring.
The beginning of life;
Time means everything.
Our parents grow older,
Dreams vanish away;
Time teaches us its lesson:
Nothing stays forever the same.

Time gives us its pleasures,
Steals hopes, dreams, and fame.
In time we surrender,
Even the memories we share.
So, celebrate time spent with loved ones,
Time is a gift God freely gave
Eternal life, Jesus died, rose and delivered;
Time becomes forever and passes away.

Esther Schultz Connor

True Contentment

Contentment together with godliness
Is great gain, the Bible says.
The blessings of the Lord make rich
And drives all cares away.
God's love divine empowers
And banishes all fear.
Be strong, stand firm,
Wear the whole armor of God,
To withstand in the evil day.

Contentment lies in the scriptures,
God's Word makes it very clear.
Learning, patience, and comfort
Fills our hearts with hope and cheer.
With one mind and mouth, we sing God's praises;
For His mercy, we glorify His name.
We are filled with joy and peace,
For in Jesus Christ we believe;
True contentment, full of goodness and grace.

True contentment needs no earth frills;
It is because of Christ alone
The present state of life's long journey
Makes us rejoice in what the Savior's done.
We awake each day, a new beginning,
Forgiven, righteous, our victories won.
Nothing else on earth can compare
With the peace, joy in Jesus we found.
True contentment, our future is heaven,
We are redeemed and not earthbound.

True Love, Pure Love

God's Word tells us to love Him
With all our hearts and souls;
To trust Him so completely,
To love becomes the goal.

True love, pure love,
Unconditional and real,
So easy to describe;
We each know what we feel.

To rest in sweet assurance
That God who knows our needs
Is working all things for our good;
Let love for Him now lead.

Each thought and every motive
Centers on one desire
To love God with our minds and strength;
Love burns an unquenchable fire.

Holy Spirit, Guide and Teacher,
Lead me in paths divine.
I want to do God's will;
Through me, let Christ's image shine.

True love, pure love,
Unconditional and real,
Now poured out freely
To love God and do His will.

Esther Schultz Connor

Trust Him Fully

PROVERBS 3:5-6

God has done so much for us,
Can we refuse when He asks for our trust?
When we seek Him only in distress,
Call frantically on His name,
He hastens to answer and deliver,
He never changes, He's always the same.

He asks for our trust, with all our hearts,
We cannot withhold, not even a small part.
He is our Savior, Redeemer;
On Him, we can depend.
He holds back nothing from us,
His only Son, willingly God sent.
To die in disgrace, to receive spittle in His face
When Jesus by His power, that day at any hour
Could summon Angel legions to deliver.
Instead He died, and our sin debt was erased,
Because God our Father offered mercy and grace.

Make your home in our hearts, Lord,
We give you our love in return
For peace and joy no one could destroy.
These are the lessons we have learned;
Let us now believe, and receive Him gladly,
Give Him full control of our hearts and our lives
To accept what He offers so freely;
We need His wisdom to live and survive.

Esther Schultz Connor

We yield to you Savior, have total control
Of our thoughts and our actions.
You are the lover of our souls;
We need your wisdom in all our ways,
Increase our understanding of your mercy and grace;
We trust you fully, lean on you, Savior,
Direct our footsteps, both now and forever.

Trust in the Lord

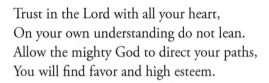

Trust in the Lord with all your heart,
On your own understanding do not lean.
Allow the mighty God to direct your paths,
You will find favor and high esteem.

Bind mercy and truth around your neck,
Write them on the tablet of your heart,
Keep God's commandments, do His will,
Fear the Lord always, from evil depart.

For good health and strength to your bones,
In your heart, let God's laws abide;
Length of days, long life you will find,
Peace reigns, like a flowing tide.

Trust in the Lord with all your heart,
From the heart, rivers of living water flow;
When you believe in Jesus and trust His Word,
The truth and its freedom you will know.

Esther Schultz Connor

Two Million Plus and Counting

To some, it may be just a number;
Untouched, they move on or turn away,
But my heart is so wounded and broken,
How can I face another day?
The days go by so swiftly, it seems;
Get on, get off, there is no delay,
You, so close to my heart, my loved one,
Was part of that awful number today.

I know I am not the only one crying,
I am heartsick and very sore,
I fasted and prayed through the illness,
That slithered inside my door.
No warning, no preparation
Was given; I looked around dazed
Before I could say my goodbyes,
You were gone; I was taken unaware.

I trust you, God; I know that you love me,
You work all things out for my good.
My finite mind finds it so hard to fathom
When an empty place lies, where love once stood.
Earthly desires, plans, schemes, and motives
Fade to dust when a loved one goes.
That is when the things of prime importance,
Take front center, God sees, and He knows.

Esther Schultz Connor

God knows the number that is growing,
He knows each one, that person's family and name.
Each one is of special remembrance
God knows how or when they came.
He sees our pain and our sorrow,
He fully understands our grief,
He is right there when we call upon Him,
Look to Him for your strength and relief.

God's Word gives us divine assurance,
The Holy Spirit is our Comforter and Friend,
He will help us to face our tomorrows.
Life begins, where some feel your numbers up, it's the end,
Now is the time to make certain our futures,
All those who in Christ Jesus believe;
There is hope for God himself promised,
Forgiveness from sin, everlasting life, they shall receive.

Unconditional Love

From you, I learned of true love
That gives expecting nothing in return.
During the time we shared together
Unconditional love's lesson I learned.
Even though you were here, for what seems a little while,
I was so blessed to have you near.
You unearthed such treasures within my heart
To love deeply someone Like you, so precious and dear.

Your sweetness, your trusting, gentle presence,
That simple, innocent smile,
Your dimples that showed on occasion,
For which I would walk more than a mile.
Some may wonder at the seeming ill fortune,
Say how sad that there is such anguish and pain,
God blessed me when He sent you my way,
God's infinite wisdom knows I would happily do it again.

Esther Schultz Connor

We Win

All praise to our loving Savior,
Our great Redeemer and Friend.
His love has no limits,
His grace has no end,
Freely poured out,
Available to all who believe,
Who exchange hopelessness,
Reaching out to receive
The free gift of life eternal,
Enduring with no end.
How to explain such love?
Such glory we can't comprehend.

God looked down through the ages
Along the corridors of time.
The struggle unending
His creation defiled.
The battles were fierce,
The victories we won.
Demonic hordes demolished
Through our Redeemer Christ the Son.
The Holy Spirit indwells us,
The redeemed by His grace.
We stand tall, daily strengthened,
By God's power winning the race.

What Christmas Means to Me

The gifts, the toys,
For girls and boys,
The presents on display, beneath the tree,
The smell of home-baked bread,
Special meals we once had
Are some of what Christmas means to me.

Although we may enjoy
Sweet delicacies and more,
Nothing compares to the real meaning of Christmas to me:
The baby Jesus Christ was born
On that special Christmas morn
To bring new life, salvation full and free.

As we rejoice and sing,
Christmas means everything.
Christ purchased on a different kind of tree;
There on a cross, Jesus was crucified,
For our sins, suffered, bled, and died,
Returned to heaven, to build mansions, for you and me.

The only choice to make,
Is Jesus, make no mistake,
He was born on Christmas Day to die, you see,
As we celebrate and sing.
Christmas to me means everything,
A gift of mercy, righteousness, and victory.

Esther Schultz Connor

When My Heart Is Overwhelmed

PSALM 61:2

When I am feeling overwhelmed
By life's dark ebb and flows,
My future looks so dim,
I don't know where to go.
My life is falling apart,
All around is worry and woe.
To the rock, I look for relief
My love for my Savior overflows.
I shout aloud, "I am blessed!
So blessed beyond belief."

When I don't know what to do,
I fix my eyes on you.
You lead me to the rock
That's so much higher than I.
I, rest and safety, know
When God is on my side.
My hands I lift in praise,
Mercy and blessings overflow;
When my heart feels overwhelmed,
God shows me the way I ought to go.

When Peace Walked In

The pressure built slowly, flooding my mind,
Consuming my heart and my soul.
Fragmented thoughts, whirling round and round,
The fears of failing, beyond my control.

The past, the present, the future loomed dark,
Failure beckoned in gloomy delight.
I seem to remember in tortuous detail,
My failures consuming the night.

So welcome the day when dawn tiptoed in;
Darkness dispelled in the rays of sun's glow.
Fears fled, smiles welcomed, as night turned to day,
Peace walked in, her calm aura in tow.

Peace sweet, slow, and wonderful,
Caressing my being, my soul,
Spreading sweet warmth, from without to within;
With outstretched arms, I release control.

God, I give you my life, I give you my all,
In your presence your joy floods my soul,
Your peace so divine, fear unwelcome departs,
Peace flowing surrounds like a scroll.

Esther Schultz Connor

Where Does the Time Go?

I hurried to enter the world,
The midwife was way too slow;
My eyes gazed around me in wonder,
On the world I was yet to know.

The sweet smiling faces of loved ones;
My childhood seemed to last only awhile,
Before I could blink or discover
I was an adult and no longer a child.

The years had slipped by; time was fleeting,
Moments jostled for place in memories' lane,
Archived and poised for remembrance,
Waiting their turn when their call came.

Life's foolish oft times wonderful decisions,
Memories and times so precious to recall;
Life holds its secrets, dreams, and visions.
Where does the time go? God knows it all.

God is my heavenly Father,
He knew me before I was born.
He fashioned my steps and my pathway,
My past, present, and future are in His hands alone.

Time lies in God's plan for creation,
Whether sleeping or awake, time moves on.
We must believe and follow God's leading
Until time is no longer and gone.

Win, Win, Winner

Win, win,
I am free from sin.
I inherit eternity,
Jesus died in my place,
Returned to heaven
To prepare a place for me.
I am a winner, for you see,
The Holy Spirit inhabits me,
That inner voice so gently speaks,
Deep down inside the heart of me.
He leads me right where I should be;
Win, win, winner,
My precious Lord and me.

Sometimes I question why
God so loved me.
His beloved Son Jesus He gave
To set me free.
His love He freely pours
On my weary, wounded soul.
My heart is fixed,
My love soars high
Where dreams exist.
A perfect union lies,
Love's sweet destiny
Here and beyond the skies,
Win, win, winner,
My wonderful Lord and me.

Esther Schultz Connor

Wipe All My Tears Away

Wipe away all my tears, God;
Your promises, they are true.
You mean what you say,
And say what you mean,
I trust you in all that I do.

This earth, this paradise, this world,
From North, South, East and West,
Your people cry out,
"Lord help us, we need you;
Please do what you do best!"

We are like children and sheep.
From your side, we have wandered away;
We should be the light and shine,
As children of God, be the light of the world,
Love God and each other and pray.

I am so happy to know
That God in His mercy did say.
He knows the heart and trials of everyone;
One day He will erase all our pain,
And wipe all of our tears away.

So, till then, I live in hope,
Peace, joy, and contentment each day.
No matter what comes and goes in my life,
If I believe His Word and trust in the Lord,
God will one day wipe all my tears away.

You Are All I Need

Joy unspeakable, blessings so sweet,
Sweeter than the honey bees make.
Your love is so wonderful, so complete;
You take all my cares away.
No one else can compare; I cannot deny,
You are perfect in all your ways.
In you, I am completely satisfied,
Thoughts of you, Lord, keep a smile on my face.

You are my beloved Savior and Lord,
In your presence, my joy overflows.
You are my Redeemer, my righteousness, my reward,
You show me the way I ought to go.
When I fall down, you pick me up,
If I stumble, you hold my hand.
You are my Comforter when tears fall from my eyes,
You whisper softly, gently, "I completely understand."

Esther Schultz Connor

You Are Always There

God, you are so awesome,
God, you are truly great,
God, you are so kind,
God, you are never late.
You show me your love, Lord,
You show me you care,
You show me your goodness,
You are always there.

Whenever I am lonely,
Whenever I feel afraid,
Whenever life's sorrows,
Fill my heart with such despair;
Whenever I need you,
My God, you are always there.
Your love is so amazing,
You answer all my prayers.

Sometimes the answer is yes,
Sometimes it may be no,
Sometimes you tell me, "Wait awhile,"
Sometimes you tell me, "Go!"
You never turn away,
You answer all my prayers;
I trust you, Lord, completely,
Whenever I call, you are always there.

You Are My Only Hope

You are my only hope,
When life overwhelms me with pain.
You are my only hope,
My future, when there is no one left to blame.
You are my only hope,
My joy when no one is there to care.
You are my only hope,
My delight, you banish all my fear.

You are my only hope,
In you I trust Lord, please take the lead.
You are my only hope,
My strength, my deliverer, all I need.
You are my only hope,
My healer, my rock, on you I depend.
You are my only hope,
My Savior, my Redeemer, and my Friend.

You are my only hope,
I look up, for my help is on the way.
You are my only hope,
You turn my darkness into day.
You are my only hope,
You give me peace, now I can say.
You are my only hope,
You are my only hope,
You are my only hope.

Esther Schultz Connor

You Are
Pretty Fantastic, God

It is so wonderful what you have done,
You are pretty fantastic God.
You sent Jesus Christ your beloved Son,
He willingly took our place,
Delivered us from sin by grace;
By grace, we are saved.
Your mercy set us free,
Free to love, free to laugh, free to live.
By grace, we are delivered
To live victoriously.

Your joy, it floods our souls,
You are pretty fantastic God;
Since Jesus made us whole,
By your will, it was done.
We are redeemed by our Savior your Son,
By grace, we are saved.
Your mercy set us free,
Free to love, free to laugh, free to live.
By grace, we are redeemed
To live victoriously.

Now we are twice your own,
You are pretty fantastic God.
Born again by the blood of your Son,
First children of Adam's race,
Then bought back children by grace.
By grace, we are saved;

Esther Schultz Connor

Your mercy set us free,
Free to love, free to laugh, free to live,
By grace, we have been bought back
To live victoriously.

You Are Somebody Special

Greatness lies deep within me,
As I know, in everyone too.
An inner sense of simply knowing,
There's more in life for you to do.
To leave your mark, your earthly footprints,
On each place, your feet have trod.
You are somebody very special,
Created in the image of Almighty God.

No other person has your fingerprint,
Your DNA is yours alone,
You are somebody so special,
Known only to God, as one day to know.
Your potential, massive thought life,
Victories won inside your head.
Of royal blood, celestial lineage,
He's God of the living, not the dead.

You look out over vast horizons,
Time's your enemy; at times a friend.
Racing headlong into the future
In whom to trust, on whom depend.
Thoughts, ambitions, dreams left unfulfilled
God Almighty, great, glorious sends.
Hope and faith, trust in His promises
To live is Christ; that's the beginning, not the end.

Esther Schultz Connor

This fleeting life is but an entrance,
An introduction to true life ahead.
A welcome center of hope and preparation,
For joys unspeakable instead.
From being earthbound, space so limited,
Quality controlled by earth's laws led.
You were destined to soar unfettered,
God's will divine, your goal, your amen.

You Complete
My Life, Lord

Give me food to eat,
I am hungry.
Give me drink, I am thirsty.
Fill me up, I am empty,
Till I am overflowed.

What you give me is temporary,
We must start over each day.
Why can't you feed me once, forever?
I have to eat today, and again.

I take a drink to quench my thirst,
"That is enough," after a while I say.
Time passes, my thirst returns,
It does not stay away.

Must I stay empty forever,
Being refueled, refilled each day.
Why is my life's satisfaction so temporary?
I need to hear what God's Word says.

"Drink of me," Jesus said.
"You will never thirst again.
Eat, I am the bread of life that satisfies."
I have waited for you, Lord, all of my life;
You complete my life in every way.

The difference, my friend, you see,
Jesus, my Lord, provides everything I need.
God sent Jesus His Son my soul to save;
Born of the Spirit, I am born again,
Forever fulfilled, my life Jesus completes.

You Have Already Won

Do not fight the devil,
Descend to his lower level.
Jesus' sacrifice removed your guilt and shame,
You are God's precious child,
Come on home, stop running wild,
Life, freedom, happiness are calling out your name.

We are aware of the enemy's tricks,
It's the old ones, he's already licked,
Trying to deceive and occupy your place.
Step right up, look up and shout,
Let God's praises fill your mouth,
Satan's lied; you have already won the race.

The battle is not yours,
Jesus Christ, He did it all.
All God asks is for you to trust and obey;
The victory is sweet.
Lay your crowns at Jesus' feet,
You have already won, so celebrate today.

Esther Schultz Connor

You Lead

Every time I think of you,
My eyes well up with tears.
Such love. Such power. Such majesty;
Your love banishes all fears.
Such love divine, so truly mine,
No human being can fill.
From dusk to dawn,
From night to day,
Keeps me secure in your will.

You are not a man,
You cannot lie,
Your promises you fulfill.
Your every thought, you think of me,
I am safe, secure in your will.
When morning comes, my hope is alive,
Such joy weaves through my day.
My soul is at rest,
I am truly blessed,
Love divine, you lead my way.

You Light Up
My Life, Lord

You, Lord, are my light;
My salvation is sure.
I trust in you, Jesus,
Your blood provided sin's cure.
You strengthen my life,
My heart knows no fear.
I gladly seek your face,
You deserve all of my praise.

Sacrifices of praise
I offer to you.
I cry with my voice,
My confidence is in you.
When enemies rise up,
Your love you make plain.
In your pavilion, you hide me;
Your tabernacle is a secret place.

I wait on you, Lord;
You are the light of my way.
Though father and mother forsake,
Your goodness brightens my day.
You take me up in your arms,
You never leave me alone.
I want to dwell forever with you,
Your beauty I desire to look upon.

Esther Schultz Connor

CPSIA information can be obtained
at www.ICGtesting.com
Printed in the USA
BVHW040625090621
609012BV00002B/267